Canyon of the South Fork of Taylor Creek in the Kolob Canyons section of Zion National Park on a clear autumn day. The Navajo Sandstone forms the vertical canyon walls, while the vegetated floor of the canyon is developed in Recent stream and pond deposits.

THE
SCULPTURING
of ZION

by WAYNE L. HAMILTON

Edited by:
Victor L. Jackson
James Staebler

Guide to the Geology of Zion National Park

ZION NATURAL HISTORY ASSOCIATION

COPYRIGHT ©1984 Zion Natural History Association
Zion National Park, Springdale, Utah 84767

Revised Edition 1992. All Rights Reserved.
No portion of this book may be reproduced in any manner
whatsoever without written permission from the publisher.

FRONT COVER
Double Arch Alcove in Kolob Canyons.
Photo by John Telford.

BACK COVER
Lone tree on canyon wall.
Photo by Edward A. Riddell.

BOOK DESIGN
Madaline Merry

COVER DESIGN
Lee Riddell, Riddell Advertising & Design

EDITORIAL PRODUCTION
David G. Ellingson

PROJECT COORDINATION
Jamie Gentry

PRINTING
Paragon Press, Inc., Salt Lake City, Utah 84101

BINDING
Mountain States Bindery, Salt Lake City, Utah

LC #78-68504

ISBN 0-915630-13-3

Guided walks such as this ➢
one to Emerald Pools give
visitors the opportunity to
learn more about the
features of Zion.

This book is dedicated
to the park visitor.
Without you our work
has no purpose.

Acknowledgments

It is with pleasure that I thank a great number of people who made this book possible: Chief Park Naturalist Victor L. Jackson who has supported the idea since its inception, former Superintendent Robert C. Heyder who encouraged me during the early stages of fieldwork and writing, Earle Kittleman for significant editorial improvements, James Staebler for pulling together the loose ends and aiding in the editorial process, Chief Ranger Malcolm S. Nicholson (Ret.) for making much of the fieldwork possible, Fred Peterson of the U. S. G. S. for help with the Jurassic stratigraphy, my father Warren F. Hamilton for timely encouragement, Zion Natural History Association board members — especially D. C. Schmutz — for their continuing support (and understanding), and most of all Assistant Chief Park Naturalist Jasper L. Crawford (Ret.) for coming up with the idea initially, convincing me that the idea was mine, and leading me along the way with his insightful and purposeful questions. I also thank Marion Hilkey for the typing, Jon Dick for many of the graphs, Debbie Sandstrom, Emily Chesick, and Tom Blaue for the art work. Meyer Rubin of the U. S. G. S. provided the radiocarbon dates. Throughout the book the photographs, drawings, and art work are attributed to those responsible, except for photos by the author and graphs.

— The "Subway", a deep canyon resembling an upside-down keyhole, was carved in rock by the rushing waters of the Left Fork of North Creek.

Tiny sand "hoodoos" capped with gravel were also carved by water — dripping one drop at a time. These are about 5 cm (2 inches) tall.

FOREWORD

The name Zion signifies various things to various people. Mostly it stimulates the mind with expressions of beauty, size or power; physical features of the Park such as color, changing shadows and fantastic shapes or forms have great inspirational effect. All of these aspects are readily apparent and appreciated, yet other values — perhaps equally great, but not always recognized or understood — are the concepts of time, the process of development, and the evolution of the canyon and its rock walls with time and space. The purpose of this book is to elucidate these features and thereby to stimulate the reader's mind with inspirational concepts that might not be attained without the assistance of some background knowledge.

Stories in Stone is the title of a book by W. T. Lee written many years ago about the geological history of this same region. Although much new information has been attained since that book was written and many ideas about Zion's history have been revised during subsequent time, the appropriateness of this title to the subject at hand is, nevertheless, complete. The author of the present book, Wayne L. Hamilton, has spent nearly five years studying the geology of Zion Canyon, much of it as geologist for the National Park Service. He contributes considerable first-hand information in this volume. Descriptions of his personal observations of the rock record and the processes involved in erosion and crustal

movements are both vivid and convincing. Not only does he treat controversial hypotheses, as well as accepted facts, throughout the discussions, but he also documents and illustrates his statements. Further, where interpretations disagree, he commonly presents both points of view.

This book has been organized into five parts or chapters, arranged to treat the most obvious and readily understood features first, and those subjects requiring relatively detailed explanation, later. Interpretations involving some background in science are largely in the later chapters. This arrangement is nearly opposite to the traditional procedure of following a chronological sequence of historical events, but is justified on the grounds that an understanding of these processes makes easier a comprehension of the more complex story that follows.

Actually the book is far more than the guide that its title seems to imply. It describes in detail and illustrates well the three basic processes that have largely controlled the Earth's form and development throughout time: 1) The wearing down of elevated areas through erosion, 2) The filling up of low areas by sedimentation, and 3) The raising or lowering of all areas by crustal movement. Chapter II is largely devoted to the various agents responsible for the erosion of the elevated land and directs the reader to places in and around Zion where excellent illustrations of various forces of disintegration and decomposition can be documented and examined in detail.

Chapter III, titled *Mesozoic History,* describes the record of Zion's rock layers in relation to Earth's history, establishing their position as intermediate between older rocks of the Grand Canyon to the south, and younger strata of Bryce Canyon to the northeast. Zion's rocks are shown to have formed during the great "Age of Dinosaurs" and to consist of a series of nine or more formations (layers) composed largely of sand, mud, and carbonate deposits. In terms of changing environments these deposits represent climates ranging from moderately humid to very arid or desert-like, and elevations ranging from shallow marine to various terrestrial situations. The author sets out an explanation of the constant changes with time and space in terms of the currently developing geological concepts referred to as "plate tectonics". Thus, variations in climate, evolution in plant and animal life, and changes in relation of land to sea apparently are largely explained by the positions and movement of segments or plates on the Earth's surface. However, Dr. Hamilton carefully points out that at this time many details of the concept, especially as applied to this region, are still only poorly understood.

The subject matter of Chapter IV, deformation of the Earth's crust, is perhaps the most difficult for the nongeologist to understand and involves many controversial matters even for geologists. The complexity of compressional and tensional forces, the resulting structures known as joints, faults and folds, and the relation of these structures to volcanism, erosion and other features of the landscape are discussed in this chapter. In brief, the events of the last 60 million years in the Zion region have been largely initiated and controlled by these deformational structures.

The lay reader of this book will be pleased to know that considerable effort has been made to explain technical terms and concepts throughout. Not only is a detailed glossary furnished at the end, and many processes such as the method of dating rocks explained at appropriate places, but also interesting and understandable comparisons are numerous. For example, plate movement on the Earth's surface is illustrated by "slabs of ice on a windswept pond," rifting of the Earth's crust is compared with "linoleum laid over a sagging floor," and an anticline is aptly referred to as a "wrinkle in a rug sliding over a slippery floor."

A final but very important feature of the book that certainly should not be overlooked is the Road Guide that forms Chapter V. Four routes and many of the areas discussed in the text are included. This section gives reality to the whole and the visitor to Zion is strongly urged to take advantage of it.

— *Edwin D. McKee*

Water forms haunting sculptural shapes and deep potholes in rock, such as these in the Left Fork of North Creek (opposite).

Cavities only a few inches in diameter, created by gases boiling out of cooling molten basalt, here form a miniature landscape.

CONTENTS

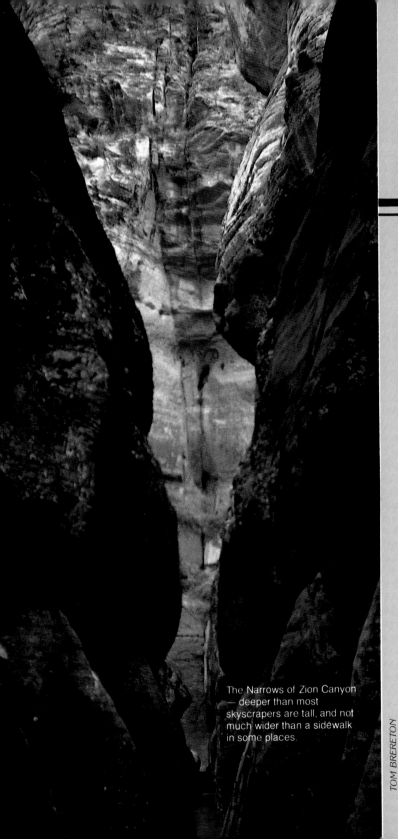

The Narrows of Zion Canyon — deeper than most skyscrapers are tall, and not much wider than a sidewalk in some places.

TOM BRERETON

3 *MESOZOIC HISTORY* *69*

4 *HISTORY OF DEFORMATION* ... *89*

5 *ROAD GUIDE TO GEOLOGY* ... *103*

Cross-bedded sandstone near the East Entrance supports large "hoodoos" (opposite), strange structures eroding under water-resistant rock caps

INTRODUCTION

The plan of this guide to the geology of Zion National Park is to deal first with the more striking, present aspects of Park terrain and secondly with the less obvious historical aspects. Therefore the first chapters deal with the origin of the rockscape as we now see it, for example the "checkerboarding" of Checkerboard Mesa and the intricate erosional dissection of the Markagunt Plateau. The present canyon and mesa environment is then traced back through time for a few tens-of-thousands of years, uncovering evidence that gives us glimpses of how the canyons were formed. There are many fascinating aspects to this backtrack through time and the evolution of these canyons, including enormous rockslides, sizeable lakes, fiery volcanic eruptions, and climatic change, each of which has left its own geological traces as well as an imprint on the topography.

The geological history can be traced back in this way for only a relatively short time before the record becomes obscured. Direct evidence of the events that occurred here from mid-Pleistocene back to early Cenozoic times* is lacking because the record has been erased by erosion. At this point, however, it is hoped that the reader will have acquired enough of a feeling for the ongoing and recent geological processes (and their

---

*Specialized terminology is defined in the Glossary.

universality) and the associated kinds of sediments (with their characteristic structures) that it will then be possible to move back in time 100 million years and more to the Mesozoic Era to explore the origins of the ancient rocks of Zion which are very much in evidence here.

The second part of the book deals with the lithic framework of the Park, the bedrock upon which the marvelous erosional sculpture has been recently executed. It is hoped that, to paraphrase LaVan Martineau, "the rocks will begin to speak". When it becomes possible to look at the cross-bedding in the Navajo Sandstone and see dry wind relentlessly moving a carpet of sand across a Jurassic dune desert, a major goal of this book will have been attained.

Although an effort has been made to define new terminology as it is used in the text, I have not always been successful in this regard. Therefore the nongeologist may find it necessary to refer to the Glossary.

Also included in the Appendix is a geological time scale which, it is hoped, will put geological time into perspective. Large numbers are difficult to comprehend, especially when they represent long periods of time, therefore it is convenient to refer to a diagrammatical time scale to see how exceedingly long Earth has existed and how infinitesimally short is the human lifespan. The time scale reveals how sketchy geological knowledge is as we consider more ancient times.

Readers with some geological background will be able to use the Road Guide for a quick overview, and refer to the text only where more detail is needed.

Finally it is most strongly recommended that the "Geological Map of Zion National Park, Utah" (Hamilton, 1978) be used in conjunction with this book. While I have attempted to make the book stand alone, the map will clarify many points on which questions may arise.

V. L. JACKSON

Fig. 1
Aerial view of the western edge of the Markagunt Plateau in the northwest corner of the Park. It is clear that streams have incised deep canyons into the relatively flat plateau surface.

THE SCULPTURING OF ZION 1

Zion is in some ways obscure and foreign, in other ways familiar and close. It is a tiny continental region on the face of the third planet of a medium-size star in one of many spiral galaxies in a universe whose extent and antiquity have yet to be determined. It is a place where a family may rest at streamside after a pleasant morning hike. It is a vast labyrinth of narrow canyons where one can become hopelessly lost, shrinking to invisibility beneath dark, towering walls of stone. One may feel triumph and exhilaration, or awesome smallness, atop Angels Landing; thirst and fatigue, or a rewarding weariness, on the return trek from the backcountry. Perhaps one's view of Zion is in the eyes of the beholder. If so, then why cannot everyone's backyard be a Zion?

Fig. 2

Cross section showing terrain and geology seen on the north (right) as one travels the Park road from the East Entrance into Zion Canyon and west (cross-country) to the West Temple. Rock formations are identified from oldest to youngest as follows: Ŧm, Triassic Moenkopi; Ŧc, Triassic Chinle; Ŧmo, Triassic Moenave; Jk, Jurassic Kayenta; Jn, Jurassic Navajo; Jtc, Jurassic Temple Cap; Jc, Jurassic Carmel; and Qs, Quaternary slide debris. Recent-age slide and alluvial materials are indicated respectively by the letters "s" and "al". Steep normal faults displace formation contacts at several locations across the cross section. The location of this cross section is identified on the "Geological Map of Zion National Park, Utah" (Hamilton, 1978). Vertical exaggeration X2.

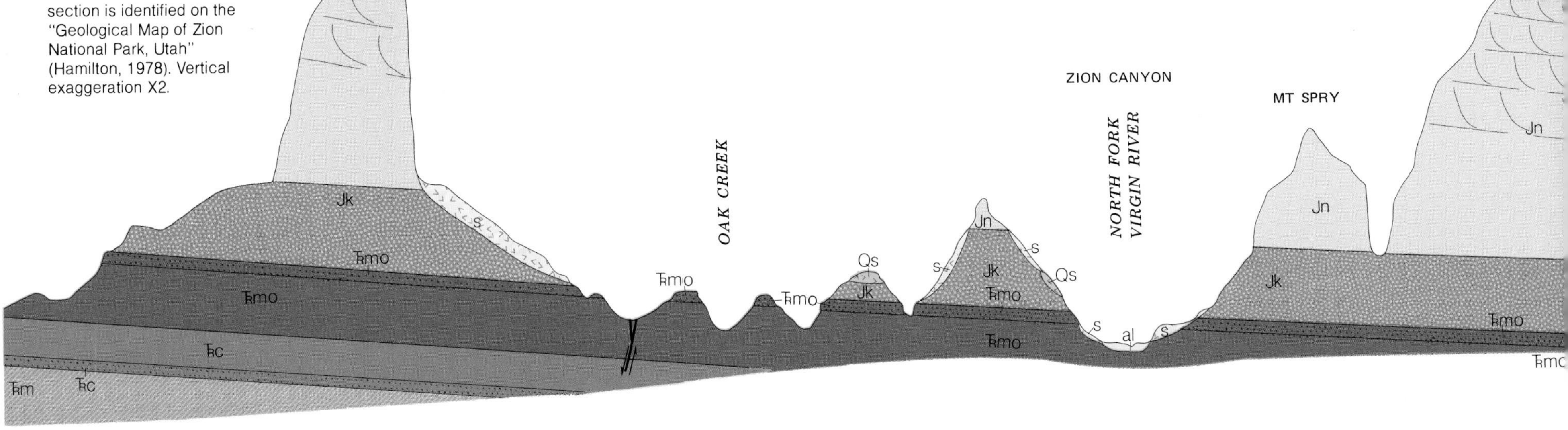

First Views of Zion

We inhabit the surface of a great living creature, Earth, whose skin, the crust, is continually being renewed. In places the land is being uplifted, and the uplift makes the surface more susceptible to the erosional processes. There are also regions where the land surface is being downwarped, and, as would be expected, these places are being filled in with sediment, the material derived by erosion from the uplifted regions.

The tendency of erosion is to make the Earth's surface level; however the energy within the Earth promotes development of a wavy surface. Since both internal and external forces operate together, a balance is achieved so that the surface is neither exceedingly rough nor everywhere very smooth.

The roughest places, mountain belts (and submarine trenches, about which I shall have something to say later), are those where interior Earth forces causing deformation (tectonic activity) are temporarily ahead, so that erosion (and deposition of sediment in submarine trenches) is proceeding rapidly, attempting to restore balance. The elevated highlands are eroded along their steepened flanks because water runs more swiftly on steeper slopes, and stream channels there develop into gullies, then canyons, if the conditions are right, cutting deeply into the bedrock. Zion is such a region, on the flank of the elevated Markagunt Plateau.

THE WEST TEMPLE

EAST TEMPLE

ZION CANYON

MT SPRY

OAK CREEK

NORTH FORK VIRGIN RIVER

Jc
Jtc
Jk
Ŧmo
Ŧc
Ŧm
s
Qs
Jn
al
Jc
Jtc
Jn

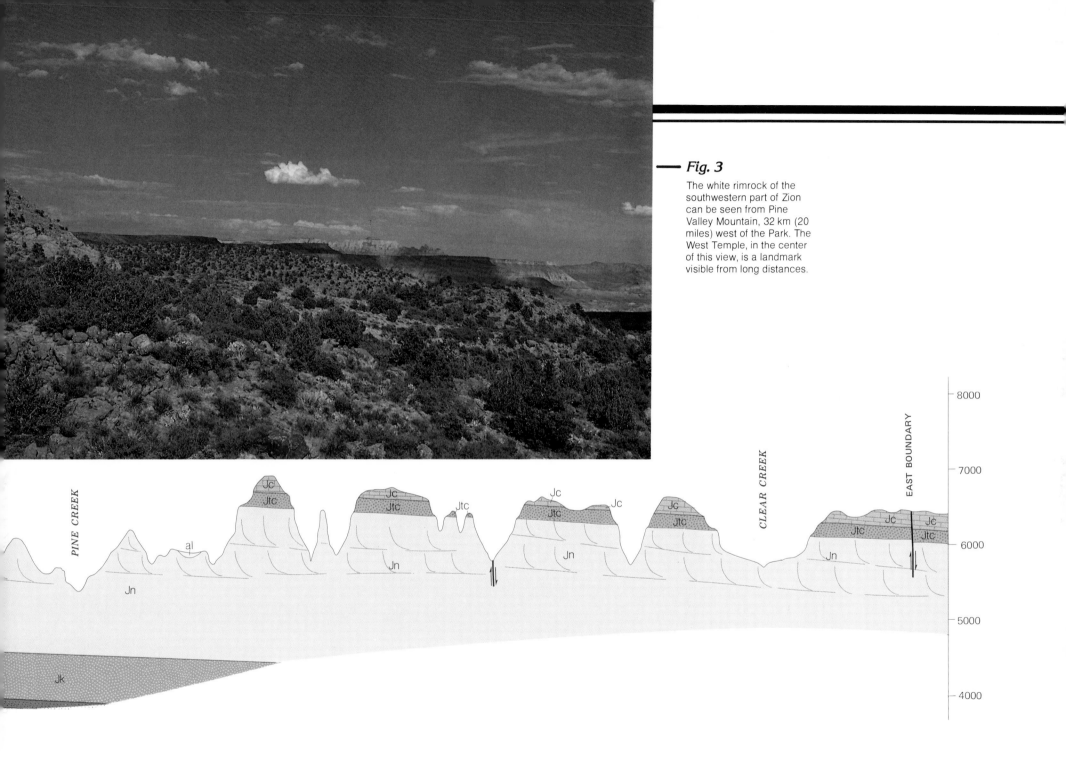

Fig. 3

The white rimrock of the southwestern part of Zion can be seen from Pine Valley Mountain, 32 km (20 miles) west of the Park. The West Temple, in the center of this view, is a landmark visible from long distances.

PINE CREEK

CLEAR CREEK

EAST BOUNDARY

Jc
Jtc
Jtc
Jn
al
Jn
Jc
Jtc
Jn
Jc
Jtc
Jn
Jc
Jc
Jtc
Jc
Jtc
Jn
Jc
Jtc
Jk

8000
7000
6000
5000
4000

It makes no difference whether you approach Zion from the east or west, the impression is that of an elevated tableland, a plateau incised by canyons. There are various levels of canyons, canyons intersecting canyons, canyons crossing canyons, and most importantly deep canyons, so that unbelievable towering cathedrals of glowing rock stand out in splendid array.

This sculpturesque terrain has been carved by erosion, literally meaning the gnawing away of rock by everyday processes operating at the Earth's surface. It takes only a glance at the cross sections to see that Zion's canyons are neither fissures nor gaping cracks nor rock crevasses, and neither are the towering canyon walls and isolated monoliths, like The Great White Throne, slabs of upthrust bedrock. The elevated features of Zion are simply the parts of this broadly uplifted and tilted plateau that have not yet been eroded away, and they exist because streams have carved deep channels into the plateau to form an intricate network of canyons.

How the sandstone, mudstone and limestone of Zion came to be here and how these layers of ancient sedimentary rock were subsequently elevated into the domain of rapid erosion will be taken up in later chapters. It is sufficient in this first view to consider Zion as an unrivaled erosional sculpture on the surface of the Markagunt Plateau, etched in layers of Mesozoic sedimentary rocks, and to explore the reasons why this is so. It is not in the least disappointing to me to realize that these canyons are not the result of titanic earth-rending forces. In fact, it is somehow more spectacular to see that ordinary processes, like flowing water, freezing and thawing, and a rock rolling downhill, have accomplished this task. One of the greatest lessons of geology is to find that given enough time, very weak forces can accomplish much.

Fig. 4

Cross section showing terrain and geology seen to the east (right) as one proceeds from lower Zion Canyon northward into the "Narrows". Formations are identified by the symbols defined in Figure 2. The location of this cross section is identified on the "Geological Map of Zion National Park, Utah" (Hamilton, 1978). Vertical exaggeration X2.

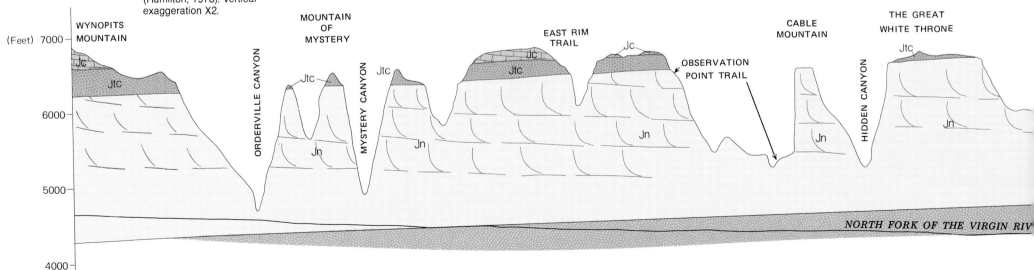

CARMEL FORMATION

TEMPLE CAP FORMATION

NAVAJO SANDSTONE

KAYENTA FORMATION

MOENAVE FORMATION

J. L. CRAWFORD

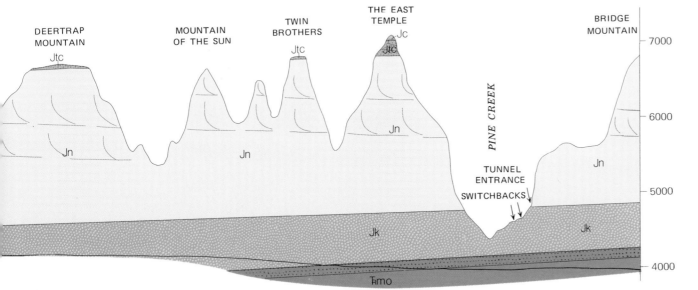

DEERTRAP MOUNTAIN

MOUNTAIN OF THE SUN

TWIN BROTHERS

THE EAST TEMPLE

BRIDGE MOUNTAIN

Jtc

Jtc

Jtc

Jc

Jn

Jn

Jn

Jn

Jn

PINE CREEK

TUNNEL ENTRANCE

SWITCHBACKS

Jk

Jk

Ŧmo

7000

6000

5000

4000

Fig. 5

View eastward from the top of the West Temple. The important rock formations are identified along the margins. The white rimrock on the horizon is Navajo Sandstone forming the escarpment along the Sevier Fault near Mt. Carmel. The Great Arch can be seen near the center of the photograph, and the Visitor Center is visible in the right foreground.

Climate and Hydrology

Climate

Because the terrain is a product of weather to a great extent, it will be useful to begin by looking at the climate of the Park. The lush green vegetation adorning the floor of Zion Canyon belies the fact that this is, at lower elevations at least, a subtropical desert where precipitation is scarce. At Park Headquarters the average annual precipitation over the period 1928-1980 was 387 millimeters (mm) (15.23 inches). The annual amount is quite variable from year to year which is a characteristic of semiarid climate. The wettest year of record, 1978, brought 1.7 times the average amount while the driest year of record, 1956, brought only 0.21 of the average. Most of the watershed of the Virgin River lies outside the Park at higher elevations. Maddox (1977) has calculated the mean annual precipitation in the North Fork of the Virgin River watershed for the period 1970-1975 at 612 mm (24.1 inches).

The precious moisture arrives in two different ways, from summer thundershowers and winter frontal storms. In summer the zone of tropical easterly flow (air moving from the east) moves northward into the southwestern U.S., occasionally bringing moist air from the Gulf of Mexico our way. If ground heating produces sufficient convection, and if the upper air is moist enough, towering cumulus clouds develop and rain falls. At other times, moist Pacific marine air moves toward Zion, bringing similar results.

In winter Zion is under the influence of the belt of westerlies, and fronts formed between cold polar air and warm, moist Pacific air sweep across the area. In this case there is an orographic effect, and higher elevations receive more precipitation than lower ones. It is typical to find about three feet of snowpack at Lava Point in the spring. On the floor of Zion Canyon most winter precipitation falls as rain, and snow seldom stays on the ground more than a day or two.

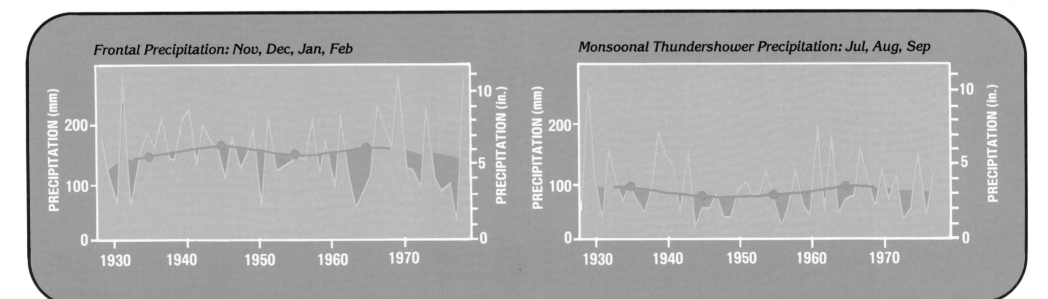

Thundershowers and flash floods are the Park's prime "earthmovers".

ROY GIVEN

Fig. 6

Precipitation records at Park Headquarters, 1928-1978. Winter (November through February) and summer (July through September) precipitation are shown separately because they affect the Park differently. Winter precipitation accumulates as snow and soaks into the ground on the high plateau, providing a continuing supply of water, via subsurface flow, to springs which feed the Virgin River and other streams. Summer rains, as thundershowers, often cause flooding and erosion, Notice that the drought of the Seventies was the worst recorded in Zion. It was due primarily to lower than average winter precipitation.

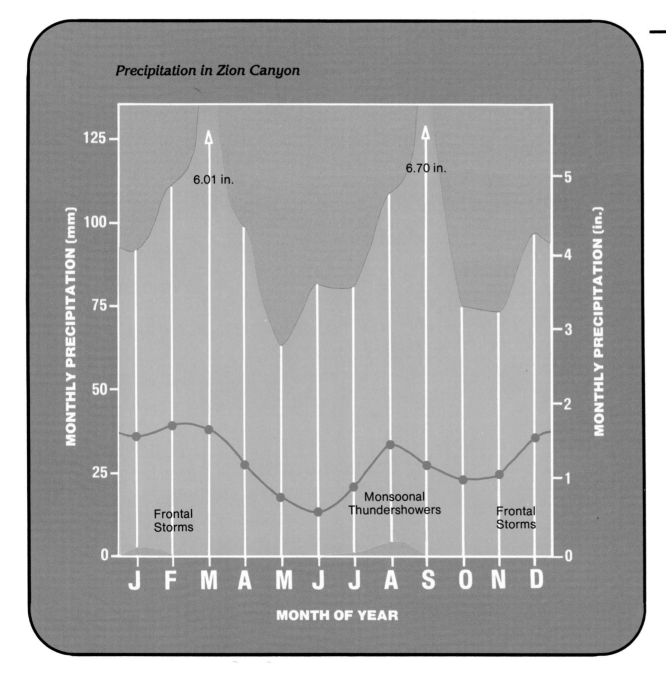

Precipitation in Zion Canyon

6.01 in.

6.70 in.

125

100

75

50

25

0

MONTHLY PRECIPITATION (mm)

5

4

3

2

1

0

MONTHLY PRECIPITATION (in.)

Frontal
Storms

Monsoonal
Thundershowers

Frontal
Storms

J F M A M J J A S O N D

MONTH OF YEAR

This bipartite climate produces two precipitation maxima annually, on average. Thundershower activity predominates in August (37 mm [1.46 inches] average for the month at Headquarters), while the frontal precipitation maximum usually falls in about February or March (42 mm [1.67 inches]). The winter precipitation, especially that falling as snow at higher elevations, is responsible for maintaining the flow of ground water, springs, and streams in this area. Snowpack that infiltrates gradually into the ground at 2,400 meters (8,000 feet) elevation insures the maintenance of healthy vegetation on the canyon floor some 1,200 meters (3,900 feet) below. Summer rain does not soak into the ground to any great extent, and it often produces flash floods at lower elevations, of little benefit to riparian vegetation.

Summer temperatures are high in the canyon, but winters are mild. The July average maximum is about 37°C (99°F), and the average January low is about -2°C (28°F). Because of aridity the humidity is low, thus in July the average daytime-nighttime temperature difference is 17°C (30°F). The difference is somewhat less in January, 13°C (23°F).

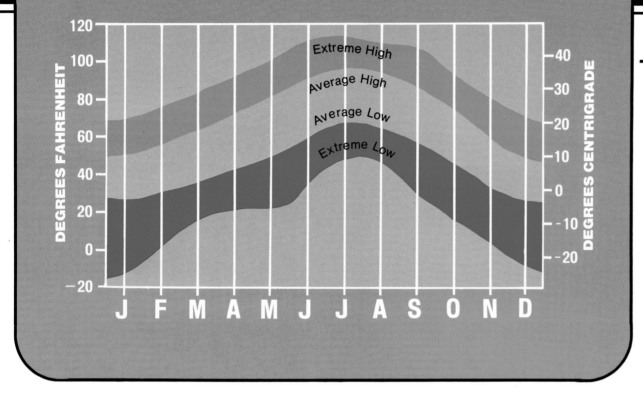

Average and Extreme Temperatures Based on Record from 1928–1969

DEGREES FAHRENHEIT

Extreme High
Average High
Average Low
Extreme Low

DEGREES CENTIGRADE

J F M A M J J A S O N D

Fig. 8

Average high, average low, and extreme temperatures by month at Zion National Park Headquarters.

returns through the canyons to the desert. The downcanyon flow hugs the ground more closely than the upcanyon flow, hence it is a much stronger wind. Shaking tents attest to a velocity of from 30 to 50 kilometers per hour (20 to 30 mph) through the campground many a summer dawn. Anyone camping a few hundred feet above the floor of a canyon would find the summer nights uncomfortably hot however, because the ventilation provided by the night wind is missing.

Hydrology

Some of the moisture falling onto the surface of the Markagunt Plateau soaks into the ground and slowly filters down through the soil into the underlying rocks. In Cave Valley, for example, the infiltration amounts to less than 20 percent of the total annual precipitation.* This groundwater flows through the permeable rock layers and surficial deposits of sand, gravel and basalt. Such permeable zones that transmit groundwater are

Lava Point is almost 1,200 meters (3,900 feet) higher than Zion Canyon, so the temperatures are lower there. In July you can expect it to be 11°C (19°F) cooler at Lava Point in the afternoon and 8°C (14°F) cooler at night. This makes the primitive Lava Point Campground attractive during the summer months.

In the canyon the afternoon summer temperatures are enhanced by an "oven wall" effect, due to the intense heating of rock by the sun. Some of the heat is dissipated by the gentle winds that move through the canyon, but when the wind stops, the temperature can climb suddenly by

several degrees (R. Lueck, personal communication).

The "canyon wind" is a special feature of the region, and during the afternoon and early evening a gentle breeze moves up the canyons (particularly those that are aligned so the canyon mouth faces into the prevailing wind). The afternoon breeze is produced by the rapid heating and expansion of air in the lowland desert near St. George, Utah. The air flows out of the basin and is channeled toward the highlands through the canyons. In the late evening and early morning the air moves back again. Having cooled at night over the high plateau it becomes more dense and

*More than 80 percent is "lost" through runoff, evaporation, and absorption by roots of plants.

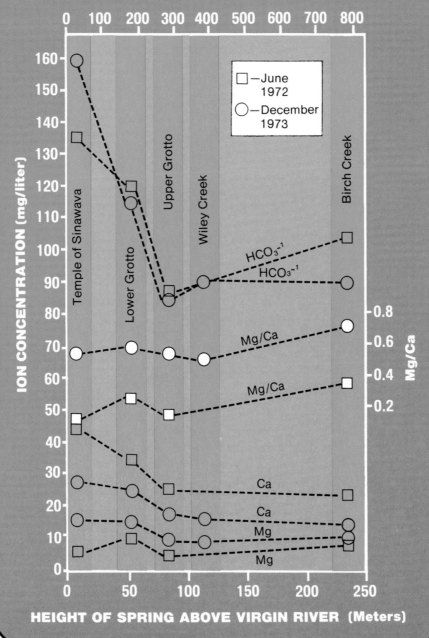

Fig. 9

Springwater chemistry in Zion Canyon. Concentration of bicarbonate (HCO_3^{-1}), calcium (Ca) and magnesium (Mg) are plotted (in milligrams per liter) against elevation of the springs above the Virgin River. In general, water quality is better at springs located farther above the canyon floor. This may be due in part to the antiquity of groundwater flow. The soluble minerals have been more completely removed from the Navajo Sandstone in the lower reaches of the canyon. The behavior of Mg relative to Ca suggests seasonal differences in springwater chemistry.

Calcium and Magnesium Concentrations, Selected Zion Springs

HEIGHT OF SPRING ABOVE VIRGIN RIVER   (Feet)

□ —June 1972
○ —December 1973

ION CONCENTRATION (mg/liter)

Temple of Sinawava

Lower Grotto

Upper Grotto

Wiley Creek

Birch Creek

HCO_3^{-1}
HCO_3^{-1}
Mg/Ca
Mg/Ca
Ca
Ca
Mg
Mg

Mg/Ca

HEIGHT OF SPRING ABOVE VIRGIN RIVER (Meters)

called aquifers, and they include portions of the Carmel Formation, the Temple Cap Sandstone, virtually the entire thickness of the Navajo Sandstone, the tongue of Navajo Sandstone within the Kayenta Formation, the Springdale Sandstone, the Shinarump, and a number of thin sandstones within the Kayenta, Moenave, Chinle and Moenkopi formations (see cross section, Figure 2).

Where erosion has cut into the land and intercepted subsurface flow, springs arise. The sustained discharge of the perennial streams in the Park derives from springs, and most springs issue from the lower portions of the Navajo Sandstone, the most important aquifer in this area.

The permeable Navajo Sandstone is underlain by impermeable siltstone and mudstone (aquicludes), so that groundwater moving downward through the Navajo, encountering these aquicludes, is forced to move laterally, forming "spring lines" where the base of the Navajo is exposed on the canyon walls. There are also impermeable layers within the Navajo Sandstone which act similarly, giving rise to springs higher up on the walls of the canyons.

After some inspection one notices that most springs in Zion Canyon are located beneath hanging canyons. Weeping Rock and its companion spring a short distance downcanyon are located beneath Echo Canyon and Hidden Canyon respectively. Grotto Springs, the Temple of Sinawava Springs, and Stadium Spring on the Gateway to the Narrows Trail are other examples.

This relationship shows that the hanging canyons and their watersheds act as areas of collection and concentration of surface water which support the springs below. Most of the ground-

12

water thus moves through only about half the thickness of the Navajo Sandstone.

Springs outside the Park maintain a small flow into the Park in La Verkin Creek, Willis Creek (left fork), and Kolob Creek (seasonally only, because a reservoir has been built in this drainage north of the Park). Larger amounts enter the Park in Deep Creek, Orderville Creek, and the East and North Forks of the Virgin River (though the North Fork would no doubt be affected by a reservoir now contemplated for construction near Chamberlain's Ranch).

Streams which arise completely within the Park are Camp Creek, North Creek, Goose Creek, Pine Creek and many smaller tributaries of the larger streams.

Little is known about the seasonal variation in flow of individual springs in the Park, though it would be most interesting to see if Weeping Rock, for example, increased its discharge in response to winter precipitation falling in Echo Canyon. It would be very nice to know how long it takes for a molecule of water to pass through the Navajo Sandstone before surfacing again at a spring in the canyon. It is known in a general sort of way that over the watershed of the Virgin River spring discharge gradually decreases in response to periods of extended drought, but the response time of the aquifer is not known as yet.

The chemistry of springwater is important in that it may influence the distribution of aquatic organisms that occupy hanging garden communities and marshes. The chemical analyses that are available for springs in Zion Canyon show that water flowing from the base of the Navajo Sandstone becomes less alkaline downcanyon, decreasing from 148 milligrams per liter bicar-bonate (mg/l of HCO_3^{-1}) at the Temple of Sinawava Spring to 98 mg/l at Birch Creek Springs. The more alkaline water contains greater amounts of dissolved calcium, making it more suitable for organisms that produce calcium carbonate shells, such as mollusks. The calcium is derived in part from the dissolution of the Carmel Limestone and the carbonate cement in the Navajo Sandstone.

The springs in Oak Creek Canyon flow from the Springdale Sandstone and are even more alkaline, bicarbonate concentration being about 180 mg/l. This seems to reflect a greater removal of carbonate cement because Carmel Limestone is nearly absent in that watershed.

The chemistry of spring water samples reveals what appears to be a seasonal variation in composition. Samples were taken in June 1972 and December 1973. While there was no systematic change in the alkalinity of spring water flowing from the base of the Navajo, there was a pronounced decrease in calcium (Ca) with a corresponding increase in magnesium (Mg) concentration. For example, the ratio of Mg/Ca changed from 0.13 to 0.56 at the Temple of Sinawava Spring in only 18 months. We should try to discover the cause of such chemical "waves" because they may be important to rare mollusks like the Zion snail.

There are other springs, actually seeps, where flow is so slow that the water evaporates on the rock surface, leaving a deposit of minerals. Such seeps have formed incrustations of salt at the base of the Springdale Sandstone in Pine Creek Canyon and Parunuweap Canyon. Deposits of baking soda, formed similarly, coat the rocks in many locations in Zion Canyon. These

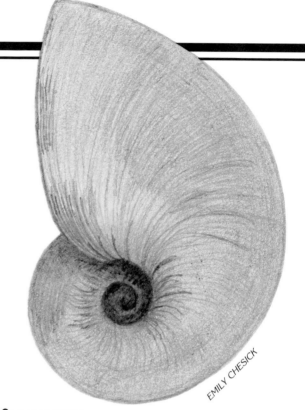

Fig. 10

Physa zionis, the Zion snail. This tiny aquatic snail is unique to Zion Canyon, where it clings to vertical wet rock surfaces at springs and seeps. The snail shown is enlarged about 25 times.

are not to be confused with the more common deposits of white calcium carbonate which have no taste.

As implied above, only a small amount of rain and snowmelt enters the groundwater system. Because of the arid climate, evaporation rates are high. Moreover plants take up some of the moisture, which is returned to the air through the leaves in a process called transpiration.

It is now time to take account of the fourth

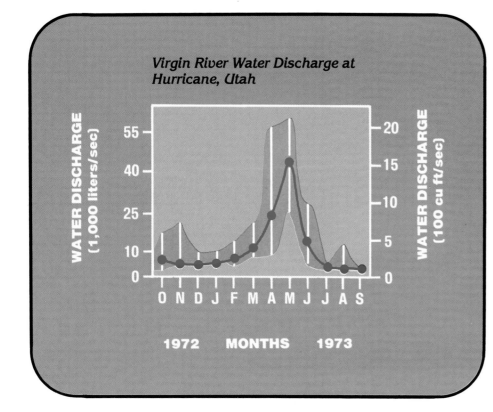

Virgin River Water Discharge at Hurricane, Utah

WATER DISCHARGE (1,000 liters/sec)

55
40
25
10
0

WATER DISCHARGE (100 cu ft/sec)

20
15
10
5
0

O N D J F M A M J J A S

1972 MONTHS 1973

Fig. 11

Water and sediment discharge in the Virgin River at Hurricane, Utah, over the 1972-73 water year (October through September), a wet year. *A)* Water discharge, in thousands of liters per second (or hundreds of cubic feet per second). Peak discharge in May was due to melting snow in the headwaters. *B)* Sediment discharge, in hundreds of thousands of kilograms per day (or tens of thousands of tons per day). *C)* Sediment discharge versus water discharge (opposite page). The data show that thundershowers move more sediment per unit of water discharge than does the runoff from melting snow.

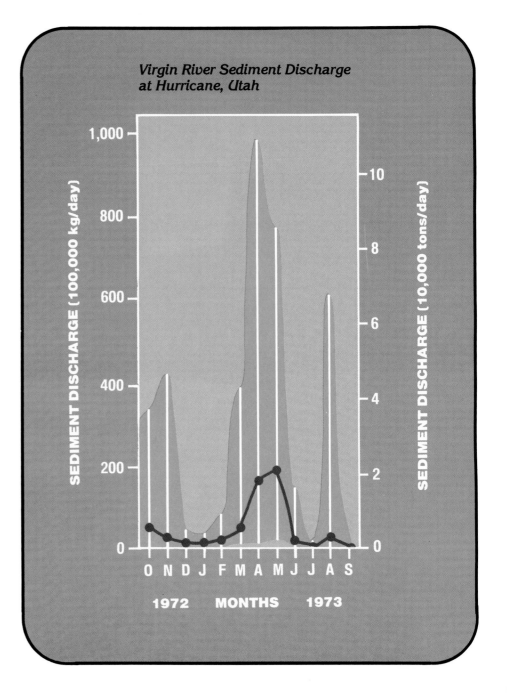

Virgin River Sediment Discharge at Hurricane, Utah

SEDIMENT DISCHARGE (100,000 kg/day)

1,000
800
600
400
200
0

SEDIMENT DISCHARGE (10,000 tons/day)

10
8
6
4
2
0

O N D J F M A M J J A S

1972 MONTHS 1973

part of the water budget, runoff. Runoff can be defined as that part of the precipitation that enters the perennial streams by flowing over the surface of the land, rather than underground. Runoff is responsible for most of the familiar erosional processes. Maddox (1977) calculated that mean annual surface runoff in the North Fork watershed amounted to 13.6 percent of the mean annual precipitation between 1970 and 1975.

When runoff is at a minimum or absent, as is the case for most of the year, the base flow of the streams (from springs) transports very little sediment. The water is nearly clear. But when there are thundershowers, or when the snow melts in the spring, runoff brings clay, silt, sand and rocks to the streams. It is typical for a ten times increase in stream discharge (water flow) to transport over a thousand times more sediment load (moving debris).

The average discharge of the Virgin River at Park Headquarters has been 2.8 cubic meters per second (CMS) (100 cubic feet per second [cfs]) over 49 years of record. Sediment discharge is not measured in the Park, but it can be estimated here from the Hurricane gaging station records at approximately 450 metric tons (500 tons) per day for a "wet" year like 1973. But extremes may be of more interest than averages. The maximum recorded discharge occurred on December 6, 1966, with a flow of 259 CMS (9,150 cfs) past Park Headquarters. The minimum of record, 0.54 CMS (19 cfs), occurred in the summer of 1977. This low flow followed a series of four winters with below average precipitation.

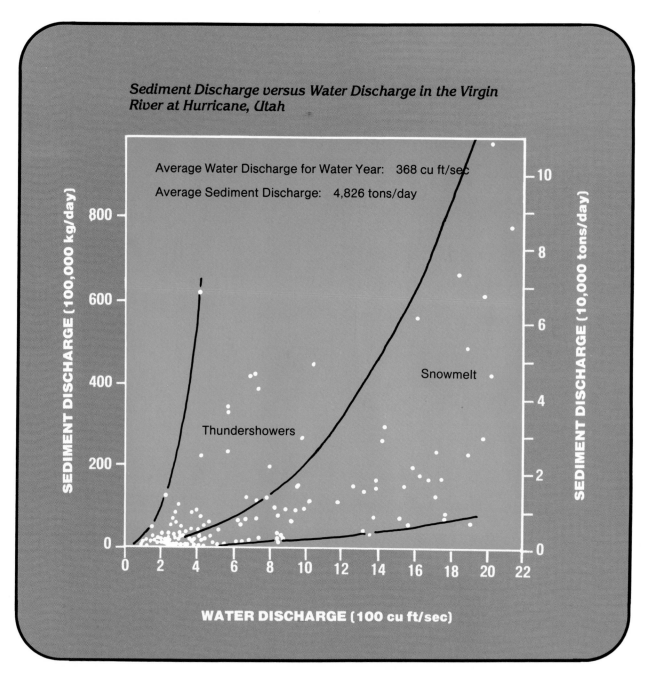

Sediment Discharge versus Water Discharge in the Virgin River at Hurricane, Utah

Weathering

Fig. 12

Weathered gravestone at Grafton, Utah. Dated stone monuments illustrate the rapidity with which stone weathers and crumbles in contact with the atmosphere and moisture. In this case water from the soil has moved upward through the stone, which acts like a wick. Dissolved matter in the water is left as salts in the pores of the rock as the water evaporates. These salt accumulations expand and cause the surface to flake away.

IN SACRED MEMORY OF

GEORGE. WASHINGTON.
GIBSON. *Born* UNION CO.
S. CAROLINA. JUNE 17th
1800.
Died AUGUST 17th
1871.

Father! thou art miss'd in Our circle.
Left Us for a better place.

WARREN HAMILTON

With the climatic and hydrological aspects of the environment in mind, it is now time to turn to the processes that affect the rocks. The first step in erosion is weathering. Bare rock cracks, crumbles, partly dissolves and becomes soil under the influence of physical and chemical processes within the general domain of the weather. The speed of weathering can be illustrated by dated stone monuments like the one shown in Figure 12. Physical weathering involves many mechanisms; however they are all characterized by the application of unbalanced forces against the grains of the rock, making it crack or crumble.

Although cracks may exist in bedrock because of previous deformation by tectonic forces, they also form when rock is exposed to the atmosphere by erosion. The pre-existing cracks, caused by regional flexing or squeezing, are called joints. Those due to gentler forces acting near the surface can simply be called cracks or fractures. The point is that all joints are cracks, but not all cracks are joints. Both will be discussed in some detail in Chapter IV.

The sandstone bedrock of Zion cracks on exposure because it is emerging from an environment below the surface where confining pressure is many times greater than atmospheric pressure. The rock mass therefore expands as it

Fig. 13 (above)

Joints in mudstone of the Moenkopi Formation in Coalpits Wash area. The case of the Brunton compass is aligned with a joint set striking north-northwest. Another set of joints aligns parallel to the compass needle.

Fig. 14 ━━━━

Superficial stresses, perhaps induced by temperature changes in the rock, produce shallow, irregular cracks which intersect bedding planes in the Navajo Sandstone at approximately 90°.

nears the surface, and cracks form, usually in planes parallel to the exposed surface. In such cases the rock is said to "exfoliate", that is it comes apart in layers like a Bermuda onion. Exfoliation is responsible for the formation of arches on these sheer rock walls (although with some special circumstances which will be described later). The expansion of the rock surface, causing slabs to break loose, is undoubtedly aided by the intense solar heating in summer.

Rocks which contain clay either as a major constituent (shale and mudstone) or in smaller quantities (siltstone and limestone) can be split apart when the rock absorbs water. Clays expand when wet and contract on drying so that shale is a notably weak rock, crumbling on exposure to the weather. Even limestone along the upper West Rim Trail and elsewhere at higher elevations in Zion has been reduced to rubble due to splitting of the rock along thin clay layers.

Water entering cracks in winter can alternately freeze and thaw. The drawing (Figure 15) shows how expansion upon freezing forces a crack to deepen and enlarge, allowing small grains of rock to settle in the crack, wedging it open. The crack can then become a niche for a plant, which by extending its roots helps to fragment the rock even further.

As cracks grow the rock becomes increasingly fragmented, exposing a greater amount of surface area and enabling weathering to proceed more rapidly, and particularly increasing its susceptibility to attack by the chemical agents of weathering. This knowledge is used by anyone

TOM BLAUE

— *Fig. 15*

Fractures are enlarged by the wedging action of growing roots (as shown in the smaller fracture), daily and yearly thermal expansion and contraction in combination with the settling of sand and small pieces of rock in the fracture, and freezing and thawing during winter (as shown in the larger fracture). Eventually, slabs of rock are pried loose by these processes.

***Fig. 16* ———**

Efflorescence of alkali in Scoggins Wash. Such accumulations of evaporite minerals are common in streambeds during the dry months in Zion. They are formed not simply because the stream dries up, but because water continues to flow for a time *underground*. Water from subsurface flow moves up to the surface by capillary action, where it evaporates and leaves behind the dissolved minerals. It is interesting to taste these minerals. Sometimes they are true "salt" (sodium chloride), but more often they taste like bitter sodium sulfate or soapy alkali.

making cake frosting because we know that powdered sugar dissolves faster than granulated and much faster than good old "rock candy".

In arid regions soil water and surface water are often insufficient to flush away dissolved matter, leaving it behind when the water evaporates as incrustations of sodium chloride (NaCl, common salt), sodium bicarbonate ($NaHCO_3$, baking soda), gypsum ($CaSO_4 \cdot 2H_2O$, alabaster), etc. As these minerals crystallize in cracks they exert a growth pressure which further fragments the rock. Such efflorescences of salt, as they are called, can be seen and tasted (for identification) along the lower trails in Zion Canyon.

Water becomes an even better solvent when it absorbs carbon dioxide (CO_2), readily available from the atmosphere or decaying soil humus, forming weak carbonic acid (H_2CO_3). The limestone found at higher elevations in Zion is literally being dissolved away in this manner. Limestone ($CaCO_3$, calcium carbonate) is carried away in solution by rainwater or snowmelt which seeps into the ground, percolating slowly down through the permeable Navajo Sandstone until it reappears at springs in Zion Canyon. Then, under the influence of growing algae and reduced pressure in the emerging water, the calcium carbonate is precipitated, coming out of solution and forming a mineral deposit called tufa. Tufa is dripstone, just like that formed in caves, and it is being deposited continuously at places like Weeping Rock and the springs along the Gateway to the Narrows Trail.

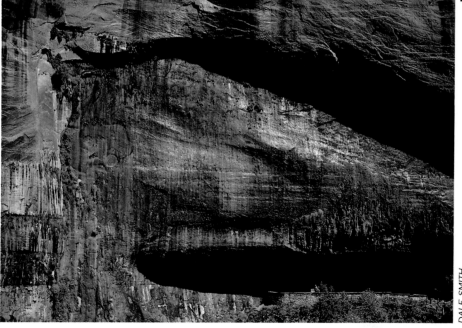

— Fig. 17

Weeping Rock, perhaps the most popular spring in Zion Canyon. Water moving downward within the Navajo Sandstone encounters an impermeable layer which directs the flow outward to the face of the cliff, where it emerges.

V. L. JACKSON

DALE SMITH

V. L. JACKSON

─Fig. 18

Lichens leave their dormant state and spring to life when rain falls. These simple algal and fungal communities lend vivid coloration to the rock surface. Red streaking on cliff near East Entrance (opposite) is caused by rain-washed hematite.

Coloration and Streaking

On a bright day the upper Navajo Sandstone and the overlying Temple Cap Formation near the East Entrance appear as yellow as lemon chiffon pie. Farther on, between Checkerboard Mesa and the small tunnel, the sandstone is nearly white, though streaked with red ochre along the mesa tops. Beyond the long tunnel and in Zion Canyon the lower part of the Navajo Sandstone is deep pink or orange-red, though here and there below seeps and spring lines it may be streaked with dull white and black, gray or tan. In other places large areas of the walls may be coated with dull black, shiny black or gray-green material. These surface colorations, better developed on the Navajo than on the other formations, have turned stark stone into an almost living thing. In certain lights the patches of darker coloration on older exposures create a reversed highlighting, and the rock masses appear to glow with an internal fire.

These colors are due in some cases to ordi-nary minerals, in others to simple plants. The Navajo Sandstone is composed primarily of white quartz sand grains cemented with white calcium carbonate, silica and a red iron oxide called hem-atite. In the upper part of the Navajo much of the cement was long ago removed under reducing conditions by flowing groundwater, causing the rock to revert to its original white color. In places the dissolved iron was redeposited and further oxidized in the presence of water to form the yel-low mineral limonite, a hydrous iron oxide. A mix-ture of limonite and hematite will appear brown.

Some of the dissolved iron was deposited in cracks and joints along with silica and calcium carbonate. Later, when the canyons were formed, slabs of rock fell away exposing large areas of these black crack fillings to view. After many years of exposure, the black coatings have become almost glassy, reflecting the blue color of the sky. This shiny black material is similar to a substance called desert varnish which forms directly on exposed rock surfaces which are intermittently soaked with iron-rich surface water. As it is often difficult to distinguish between the two (they differ primarily in their origins), I usually refer to all such shiny coatings as desert varnish. Some of it contains significant amounts of manganese, giving it a purplish hue.

The red streaks which make the Navajo mesa tops appear to drip with blood (hence the name Altar of Sacrifice) consist mainly of hematite derived by rain wash from the red shales at the base of the Temple Cap Formation at the top of the Navajo. There is a similar red shale at the base of the Carmel Formation above the Temple Cap that produces a like effect.

Streaking below spring lines and seeps is usually attributable to communities of algae and white evaporite minerals which are left behind as the mineral laden spring water evaporates. Where waterfalls occasionally wet the rock faces, mosses and lichens may form dark streaking on the walls. Perhaps the spring water is chemically unsuitable for lichens or they do not tolerate prolonged wetting for they grow well away from the springs.

Large areas of rock surface are coated with a dull black or gray-green patina of lichen. In other areas there are thick black coatings of moss. During the long, dry summer months these plants lie dormant, lending subtle tones to the red rock, but when the clouds bring rain, the walls of the canyon are instantly transformed. The dull lichens burst into vast patches of sea-green and somber black growth, and the mosses become tapestries of emerald and rich brown. Viewed close-up, there is nothing to rival the vivid coloration and the delicacy of these simple rock plants in full bloom.

ALLEN HAGOOD

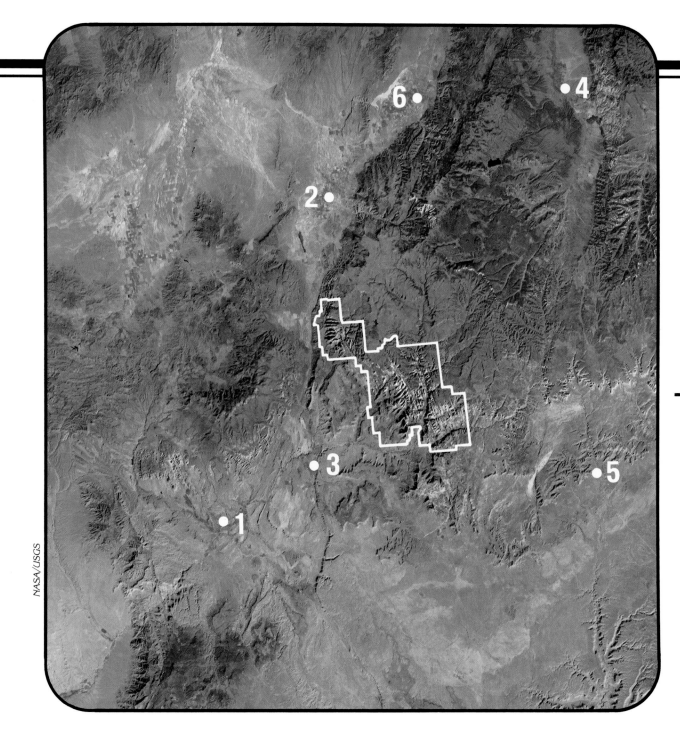

NASA/USGS

Erosion

Erosion, the removal of rock and weathered rock debris at the Earth's surface, is due to the gentle pull of gravity acting through such agents as moving water (and ice in other areas). Wind also plays a role, though not as energetically here as in Death Valley, for example. Let us now investigate the canyons of Zion to see how they have been created and shaped by erosion.

If we take Zion Canyon as a typical example

Fig. 19

Satellite photograph of Zion National Park and vicinity on October 27, 1979. The Park boundaries are shown in the center. The red represents dense green vegetation. Lakes and reservoirs appear black. Lava flows appear dark gray. Town locations: 1) St. George, 2) Cedar City, 3) Hurricane, 4) Panguitch, 5) Kanab, and 6) Parowan. Photo by NASA/USGS EROS Data Center, Photo ID: 82173917273XO

Fig. 20

An aerial view looking southeast across Zion Canyon and the eastern portion of the Park shows a profusion of joint-controlled canyons.

we see that at Park Headquarters it is about three or four times wider than it is deep. At the Temple of Sinawava the width and depth are about equal. If you follow the canyon upstream from there into the Narrows, you will see that there are many places where the sheer walls are several times higher than the width of the gorge. In fact, there is one place where the Narrows is only about 5 meters (16 feet) wide at the bottom of a 300 meter (1,000 feet) deep slot. These statistics show that we should consider erosive downcutting and widening separately because they operate at different rates in different parts of the canyon and in different kinds of rock. W. K. Hamblin and others (1975) have shown, for example, that in the soft Kayenta shales near St. George the Virgin River has accomplished over six times more widening than deepening in the past million years or so. On the other hand it is obvious that downcutting is proceeding much more rapidly than widening in the Narrows.

Downcutting

A river cuts down through bedrock by scouring away materials loose enough to be dislodged and by abrasion, where fragmented rock material is impacted against the streambed by turbulent flow, literally grinding down the surface. Most abrasion is carried out by the bedload of the stream, the larger detritus that is pushed, rolled and bounced along with the currrent. Bedload consists of sand, gravel and cobbles that lie idly in the streambed when the water level is low. When the river floods however, these materials begin to move, and they are transformed into a ribbon of slashing sandpaper, riding on the torrent and grinding against the bedrock underneath. Thus we see that deepening occurs quite sporadically, depending on the weather.

A glance at the satellite photograph (Figure 19) shows that Zion's canyons are arrayed in very regular patterns. The tributary canyons of the East Fork (Parunuweap Canyon) and those along the East Entrance Road are aligned in a north-northwest, south-southeast direction. The Finger Canyons in the Taylor Creek area are aligned east to west. Certainly this is not a random pattern, and it becomes evident from study of aerial photographs that most canyons in Zion have developed along joints and, demonstrably in some cases, faults in the Navajo Sandstone.

It is not always easy in this Navajo Sandstone terrain to distinguish between joints and faults.* Nevertheless, whether joints or faults, running water tends to channel along in the fractures, removing weathered debris, scouring, abrading and deepening them until finally some of them become truly canyon-size. In time a particular canyon will enlarge to encompass several or many such parallel fractures.

It would be useful to consider for a moment how it is that these canyons come to have nearly vertical walls. There are several basic require-

V. L. JACKSON

---

*The difference will be discussed later.

Fig. 21 ——————

Near the "Subway" in the canyon of the Left Fork of North Creek the stream runs along in a joint, creating an excellent example of the beginning of a joint canyon.

V. L. JACKSON

ments that must be satisfied before cliff-sided gorges can form. These are 1) rapid downcutting by the stream, 2) erosion of a relatively strong, self-supporting rock, 3) development in rock that is relatively homogeneous, 4) if heterogeneity exists in the form of joints or bedding then it helps if the joints are vertical and the bedding is nearly horizontal, and 5) development in a region with a semi-arid climate. Some examples will illustrate these criteria.

The long profile of the North Fork of the Virgin River (Figure 22) shows the streambed as if we had straightened out all meanders and set it up on a large table to view it from the side. With this side view, we see that the steepest gradient, where the water flows fastest downhill more or less, is in the Narrows of the canyon, where the walls are more nearly vertical. The same picture

Fig. 22 ——————

Long profile of the North Fork of the Virgin River between Chamberlain's Ranch and the confluence of the North Fork and the East Fork. The average drop of the stream in this sector is 13 m per km (71 feet per mile). It is noteworthy that due to recent damming of the channel by slump, and accumulation of lake and stream deposits, the river is presently cutting bedrock only upstream from Orderville Canyon and then only when the channel fill is suspended as bedload during periods of high water.

The gradient is steepest, 25 m per km (130 feet per mile), between Chamberlain's Ranch and the confluence with Deep Creek. It decreases to 13 m per km (71 feet per mile) between Deep Creek and the Gateway to the Narrows Trail and becomes even less, 6.5 m per km (34 feet per mile), between the Temple of Sinawava and the Lodge. Steepening of the gradient between Birch Creek and Canyon Junction is due to the recent blocking of the river by the Sentinel Slide.

emerges when other canyons of the Park are investigated. Rapid downcutting can produce a "canyonesque" terrain if the next criteria are also met.

The nearly 610 meters (2,000 feet) thick Navajo Sandstone is well suited to canyon development because it is strong enough to be self-supportive on a cliff face exposing its entire thickness for significant lengths of time, yet it is not so strong that it cannot be rather easily abraded by stream action. Downcutting can proceed much more rapidly than rounding-back of the rim by weathering and rockfall.

It is apparent that abrasive downcutting, acting like a bandsaw, can produce a vertical slot under these conditions, but what about Cable Mountain or the great West Temple? These vertical faces have formed well away from the erosive focus of moving water, as is evident from the sharp edges on slabs and buttresses. Somehow the verticality can persist and even become accentuated through the canyon widening process. The myriad vertical joints in the Navajo Sandstone are the controlling factor. These internal fractures are planes of weakness along which

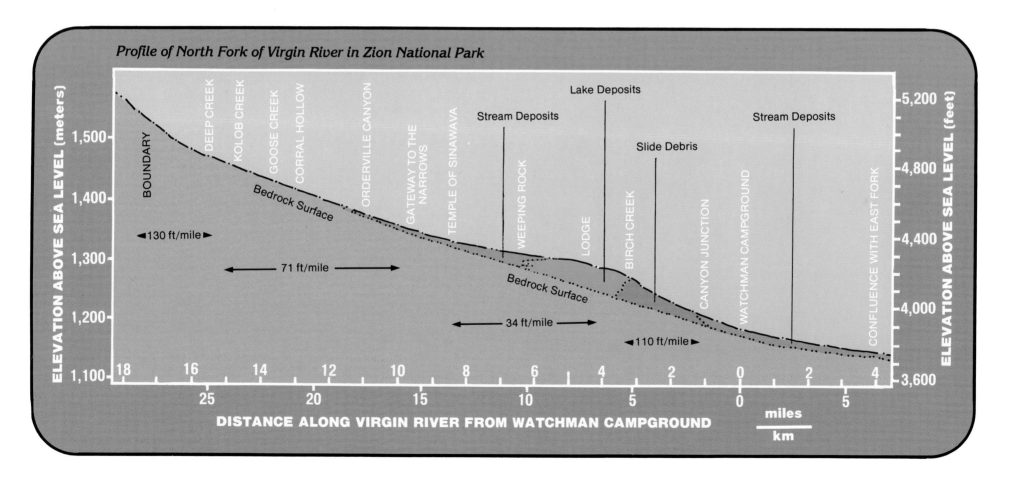

Profile of North Fork of Virgin River in Zion National Park

the rock can break and fall away, leaving sheer walls. This process will be taken up in greater detail shortly.

The typical canyons of Zion are found primarily in areas where the sedimentary layers are almost flat lying, or if they are dipping (inclined), then the direction of dip is roughly parallel to the course of the stream. Where the stream runs at right angles to the direction of dip of the Navajo Sandstone, as is the case along Timber Creek near the upper Kolob Canyons Road, then sheer walls will be found only on the down-dip side of the valley. A sloping surface will develop on the up-dip side. This occurs because the massive strata on the up-dip side can slide streamward on slippery underlying formations of unconsolidated clay and silt. There will be more to say in the next section about the spectacular results of sandstone resting on a dipping bed of mudstone when canyon cutting removes the support on the down-dip side.

If all of the above criteria were satisfied, canyon development would not proceed to the extent seen here without the arid climate. The scarcity of moisture means that vegetation does not grow as rapidly or as densely as it does in humid regions. When rain does come, soil and

Fig. 23 ━━━━━━

Record of movement of a slumping hill in Springdale, Utah, correlates rather well with rainfall. Measurements were discontinued in 1975 when it became apparent that the bench west of the hill was also moving, giving rise to anomalous negative values.

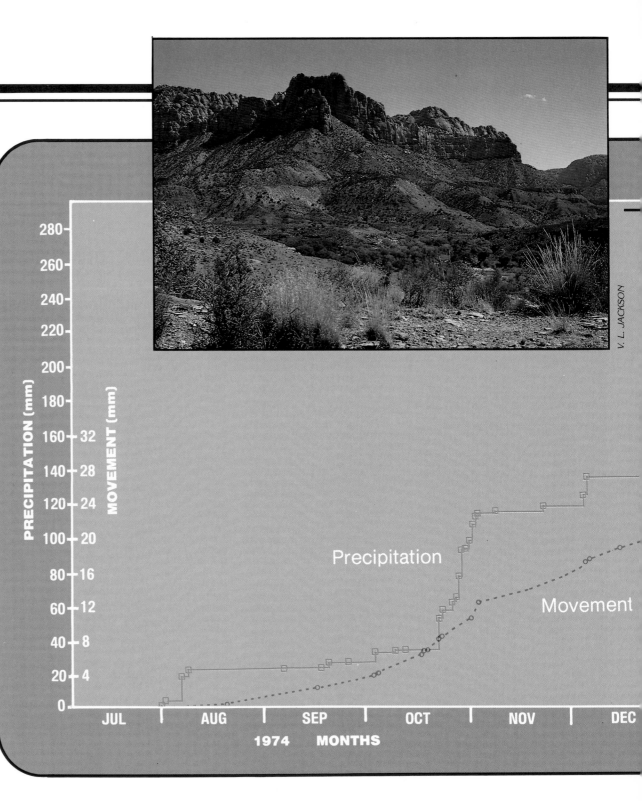

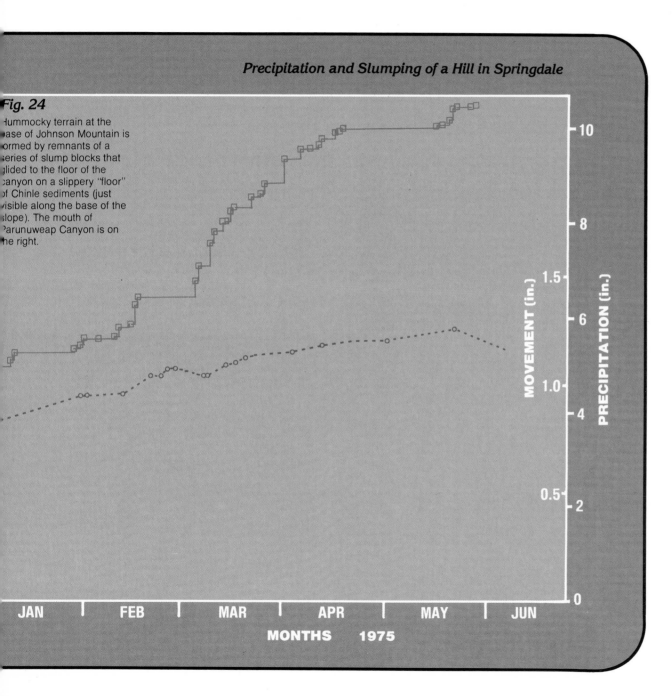

Precipitation and Slumping of a Hill in Springdale

Fig. 24

Hummocky terrain at the base of Johnson Mountain is formed by remnants of a series of slump blocks that glided to the floor of the canyon on a slippery "floor" of Chinle sediments (just visible along the base of the slope). The mouth of Parunuweap Canyon is on the right.

MOVEMENT (in.)

PRECIPITATION (in.)

JAN   FEB   MAR   APR   MAY   JUN

MONTHS   1975

rock fragments are washed into the streams, and the streams flow so violently that car-sized boulders are moved along with the current. The canyon floors are repeatedly stripped bare by episodic flash flooding. This is why talus slopes do not build up to an appreciable extent at the base of cliffs in Zion. Deep accumulations of soil and rock debris that serve to subdue the topographical relief in regions with thick vegetative cover are uncommon here.

Widening

If you hike the Narrows of the North Fork of the Virgin River, Parunuweap Canyon or the Left or Right Forks of North Creek, you will see only Navajo Sandstone walls once you leave the limestone and basalt terrain of the uplands. Only far downstream where the canyons widen will the underlying formations come into view. The rocks underlying the Navajo are the much softer siltstones and shales of the Kayenta Formation, so one sees that there is a relationship between the canyon widening process and the exposure of weaker rocks by the downcutting streams.

Several processes are responsible for canyon widening including rockfall, rock slides, mud slides and sheetwash, but by far the most effective and rapid one is slump, admittedly a lackluster term for a geological blockbuster. In canyon country where thick strong rock strata overlie incompetent rocks, the stage is set for large-scale slump when the river finally cuts through to the weak underlying strata. Slump will be even more likely if there is a gentle dip in a direction at right angles to the course of the

Fig. 25

Floods such as this one in July, 1975, although infrequent, are responsible for cutting Zion Canyon. A flooded stream discharging into the clear Virgin River (opposite) shows how much silt and sand rushing water can carry.

V. L. JACKSON

stream. Slump will become a certainty if in addition small tributary side canyons develop alongside and *parallel to* the main canyon on the updip side. The foregoing, you may now recognize, is a reasonably accurate description of Zion Canyon.

Large slump blocks, also called toreva-blocks, may glide down into the canyon. A toreva-block is a piece of the canyon wall that detaches in more or less one piece and descends, tipping back slightly as it does so, so that the bedding in the block dips back toward the sliding surface.

Such movements are not always rapid. Records of movements of a slumping hill in Springdale indicate an average rate of movement downhill of at least 3.5 mm (⅛ inch) per month. The rate of movement depends strongly on the

amount and frequency of precipitation, which apparently soaks into the ground, expanding the clays in the surface layer and pushing the hill downward. The record shows some uphill movement at times, however this anomaly occurred because the measurements were referenced to an adjacent bench uphill which, it turned out, was also moving toward the road. Certain evidence suggests that other, larger slump blocks ultimately moved much faster than this. Zion Canyon and other major canyons in the Park are replete with evidence of major slump activity, and this will be treated in some detail along with some of the effects in the next chapter.

As mentioned above, downslope movements would soon choke the floors of the canyons with the debris of mass wasting if it were not carried away by the streams. In the wider parts of the canyons such debris is rarely deposited directly in the stream channel, rather it comes to rest on the floodplain or on the slopes just above the floodplain. In this case the material can only be washed away when the stream channel migrates across the floodplain and begins cutting into the accumulated rubble. It is worthwhile to consider for a moment why it is that rivers meander and especially why the meandering channel relocates from time to time, eventually occupying all parts of the floodplain, and even enlarging it. This is an especially useful concept for those of us, the majority, who live on or near river floodplains.

The thing that causes a stream to deviate from a straight line course downhill is an obstacle. Of course moving water is a great obstacle remover, especially when the stream flows down a steep gradient; however in the downstream area where the stream has already done most of its downcutting, and the gradient is not too steep, impediments can successfully divert the flow. Obstacles can include a boulder deposited during flood stage, one that has rolled into the channel or a sandbar formed as the stream cleans and redistributes bed material after flooding. Rivers that episodically carry large amounts of mud, sand and rocks are especially prone to such blockage. The bed load which comes to rest as flood waters recede is frequently so abundant that it forms natural levees and coffer dams, choking the channel here and there and forcing the diversion of flow in other directions. This is the case with the Virgin River. U. S. Geological Survey water quality records show that the concentration of suspended solids carried by the water varies by a factor of about 500, depending on the amount of rainfall in the drainage basin. The amount of sediment transported by the river, depending on the concentration and the water discharge, varies by a factor of about 5,000, sometimes reaching 100,000 or more tons per day at the gaging station near Hurricane.

When the river seeks out new channels, adjacent slump and slide deposits can be picked up and carried downstream. In this process, what may have been a riparian woodland yesterday may become a stream channel tomorrow. An event like this inundated the Watchman Campground Amphitheater in 1966. In this case, a levee was then constructed in an attempt to make the river behave in a more civilized fashion. The National Park Service recognizes that such management efforts are doomed to perpetual maintenance, rivers being totally ineducable, however some compromises seem to be inevitable when we come to the wilderness. Alas, even the best of us leave footprints.

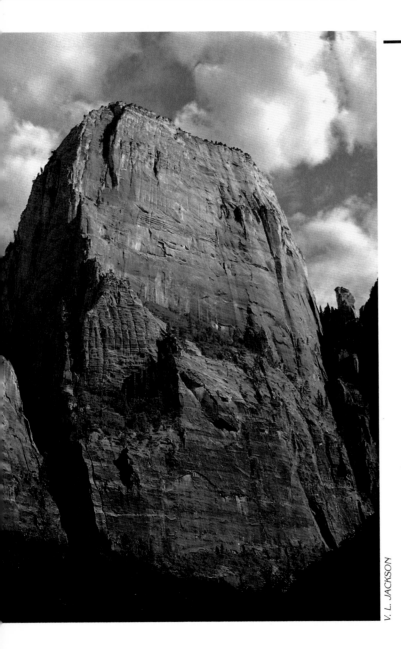

Fig. 26

The Great White Throne (previously known as El Gobernador, the ruler) derives its character from the degrading influence of weather and the pull of gravity over many millennia.

Other Results of Erosion

Zion's canyons have only a few walls that are sheer clear to the top of the Navajo Sandstone. In most areas, like the canyons of North Creek, Pine Creek and Zion Canyon, the rock has acquired a degree of rounding-back near the top that greatly enhances its beauty. The Great White Throne for example is not a pure geometric form like a rectangular prism but more worn at the top like a well-used Artgum eraser. The North and South Guardian Angels are even more beveled giving them the appearance of colossal dips of soft ice cream. The rock seen close up exhibits fantastic fluted, castellated and cavernous forms that challenge comprehension. This subdued aspect of the rock, the gentled surface of the upper portion of the Navajo Sandstone, gives Zion a special degree of warmth and brings what would otherwise be a harsh landscape into pleasing harmony with the shapes of trees and sky.

There is a *bona fide* geological explanation for this extra measure of erosion in the upper levels of the Navajo and on sandstone surfaces long exposed to weather. In the places where the rock takes on a subdued relief and a rounded grotesqueness, the sandstone is whiter, browner or yellower than elsewhere. This coloration differ-

ence is an indication that the original cementing materials, including the red mineral hematite, have been largely dissolved away by groundwater, freeing the quartz sand grains. Once freed, the grains fall away from the rock under the influence of gravity or pounding raindrops or later, when a gentle puff of wind arrives. This type of sculpturing results in the smoothed, rounded and fluted rock surfaces so commonly seen over much of the higher sandstone terrain in the Park.

Intricate recesses, some looking like miniature cliff houses or fairy caves, form on exposed joint surfaces. Deep within the rock, groundwater once partially filled many of the pre-existing joints with mineral precipitates like silica, calcium carbonate and (as previously mentioned) iron minerals dissolved from the rock at higher elevation. When later exposed by development of the canyons and subsequent rockfall, these exposed surfaces suffer varying degrees of weathering, depending on the thickness and kinds of joint filling minerals. Some coatings, like desert varnish and silica, are resistant to chemical weathering and protect the rock surface for many centuries. Eventually, however, rainwater finds a weak point in the veneer and removal of calcium carbonate cement behind the covering begins, followed by the excavation of sand grain-by-grain due to the incessant pull of gravity aided by rain

Fig. 27

A view from the West Rim Trail into the upper canyon of the Left Fork of North Creek. The notch to the right of center is Guardian Angel Pass, flanked to left and right respectively by the South and North Guardian Angels.

and wind. In time these grottos develop with great diversity as seen in Hidden Canyon, Refrigerator Canyon and places along the Gateway to the Narrows Trail.

The removal of much of the iron mineral from the white upper Navajo may have occurred through the reducing action of liquid hydrocarbons moving with groundwater shortly after those sands were originally deposited. Today this rock is notoriously crumbly, dangerous from the standpoint of rock climbers and so weak that even lichens cannot grow fast enough to establish a secure hold on it. Where the upper Navajo is still cemented, as in the Finger Canyons, the walls are near vertical and red all the way to the top.

Surfaces like the face of Checkerboard Mesa and other exposures seen from the West Rim Trail are another special case of gentle erosion in Zion. These "waffled" surfaces are due to a pattern of nearly vertical cracks superimposed upon almost horizontal layering in the sandstone. The layering is a result of sedimentary processes that will be discussed later, and it is fairly easy to see how coarser layers (those containing larger sand grains) can be more easily decemented by rain water, producing the sets of nearly horizontal grooves.*

The near vertical set of grooves is more challenging and requires study. On close examination it appears to consist of fractures from which sand has been removed by weathering and erosion.

*Coarser aggregates are more permeable to water, and larger grains are more susceptible to the pull of gravity because they are bound less tightly to the rock by electrostatic bonds, for the same reason small dust clings more tenaciously to your car than does sand.

The fact that the fractures seem to be shallow, that they are at right angles to the coarse-grained layers and are arrayed in a radiating pattern around Checkboard Mesa shows us that they are not joints. Their origin is not related to regional deformation, but to something that is deforming the mesa at the present time. This superficial cracking may be due to expansion and contraction in the surface layer of the rock that causes failure of a type quite different from exfoliation. The expansion and contraction may be caused by solar heating (and cooling at night), or freezing and thawing of the snow soaked surface during the winter months, or, as suggested by G. Holdsworth of the Canadian Geological Survey (personal communication), perhaps simply wetting and drying. Holdsworth has shown quite convincingly that expansion and contraction in the surface layer would, because of the existence of a set of weak horizontal layers, produce a set of fractures cutting across the weak layers at right angles. Moreover, the spacing of the vertical fractures would be about the same as the spacing of the horizontal ones if the expansion/contraction occurred rather uniformly over the affected surface.

So far no experiment has been done to check this hypothesis, nor to determine which of the proposed shrink/swell mechanisms might be most important. This would need to be done before adopting an interpretation; however the effect of temperature variations has been evalu-

Fig. 28

Cavernous weathering, the term given to such a grotesquely weathered rock surface, is the result of small differences in the vulnerability of rock to attack by atmospheric agents. The rock is more easily eroded where the intergranular cement is lacking. Calcite as a cementing medium is rather easily dissolved by rainwater or melted snow. Silica cement is much more resistant to such dissolution.

Fig. 29

Checkerboard Mesa. Sand-dune bedding structures form the nearly horizontal array of grooves. The vertical set of grooves is formed by shallow fractures caused by expansion and contraction of the rock surface, perhaps by heating and cooling.

V. L. JACKSON

TOM BLAUE

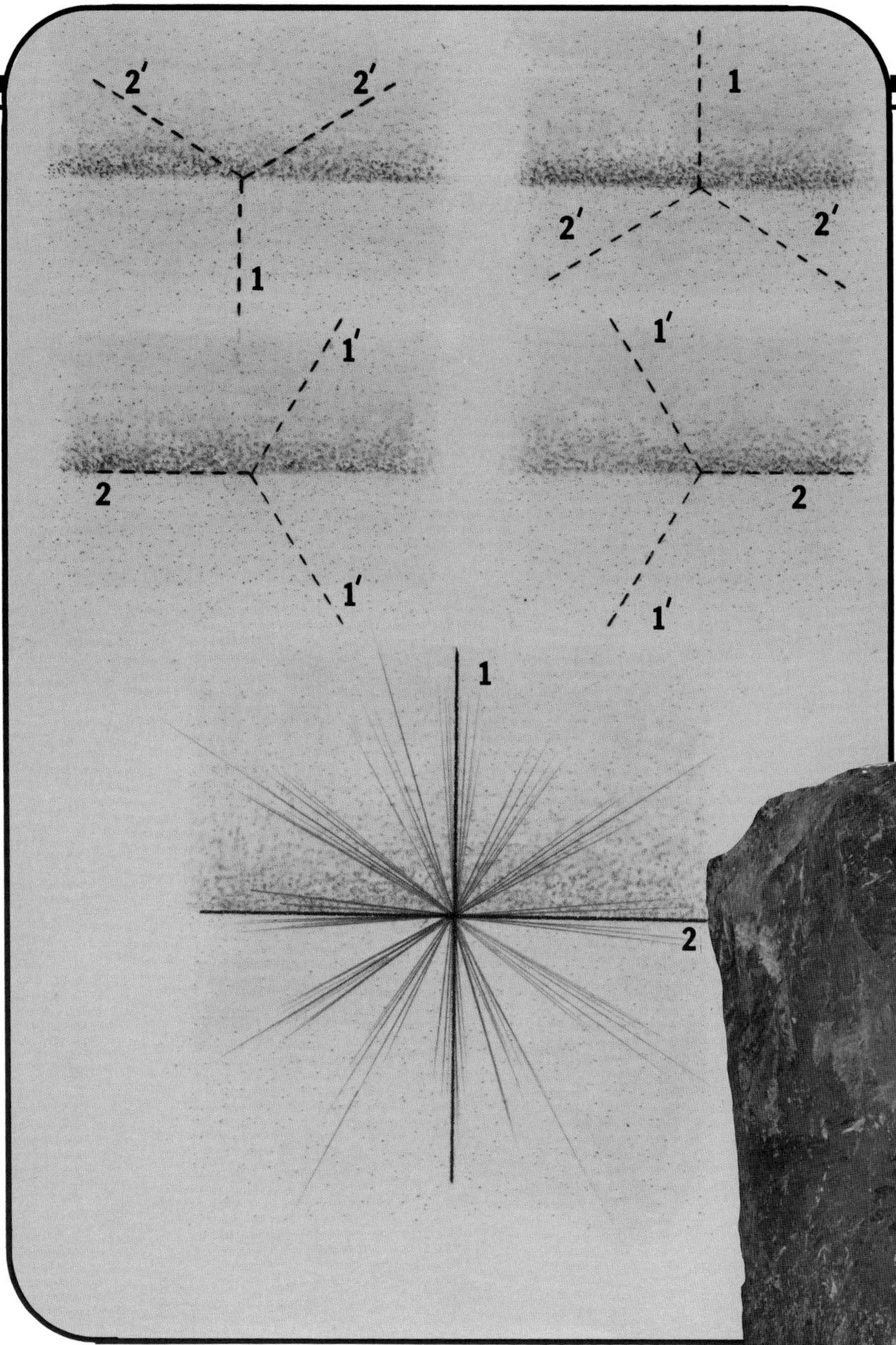

Fig. 30

Most probable stress trajectories caused by expansion/contraction in the vicinity of a bedding plane in sandstone. Bedding plane weakness promotes cracking indicated by 2. Perpendicular cracking, 1, is promoted by combining the 1' components.

Fig. 31

Dramatic evidence of the power of falling and rolling rocks. This truck was demolished by a rockfall in Oak Creek Canyon in 1947. The rock weighed an estimated 880 tons.

ated nearby. Measurements made at the cliff face alongside the Zion-Mt. Carmel Tunnel show that stress varies seasonally with the temperature by as much as 84 kilograms per square centimeter (1,200 pounds per square inch) from summer to winter.

We are accustomed to thinking of erosion as something more than the grain-by-grain reduction of a sandstone surface. Our usual conception is of weathered rock debris, including sizeable rocks, moving downslope by gravity until it comes under the influence of moving water which speeds it on its path to a new resting place. Rockfall such as this is common in Zion, and the peaceful streams and rivers can become on occasion raging torrents capable of moving huge quantities of debris very quickly (see Figure 25).

FAGERGREN

Where sheer canyon walls are found, rockfall is to be expected at any time. The accumulation of fallen rock (talus) at the base of a cliff attests to this geological hazard, particularly along the highway by South Campground. And while some rocks may fall or roll directly into the stream below, most such debris comes to rest for a time on a slope between cliff and stream. Once in the streambed, rocks will be carried downstream when the water turbulence becomes great enough, as during flood stage. If a rock is too large to be moved by even the biggest flood, then it must first be worn down to a smaller size by abrasion caused by the impacting of silt, sand and gravel carried by the current. Rocks and sand grains tend to become rounded in this way.

Fig. 32

Heavy rains in July, 1975, produced a mudflow which crossed the highway switchbacks in Pine Creek Canyon, sweeping the car shown above off the road, carrying it 150 feet down a steep gully, and depositing it beside flooding Pine Creek. Its occupants miraculously escaped injury.

Fig. 33

The largest of eleven landslides that occurred on the Emerald Pools Trail February 18 and 19, 1980. Heavy rain added to the weight on the slope and reduced the friction. Through the centuries this process moves very large amounts of weathered rock debris.

V. L. JACKSON

JAMES E. STAEBLER

The broken rocks that come to rest on slopes can be rolled downhill if disturbed by a grazing deer. Or rainfall can cause the rubble to creep, slump and slide downward toward the stream because most such slopes are formed on weathered shale or mudstone which becomes slippery clay when wet. That such slopes are quite unstable is indicated by tipped and uprooted vegetation maintaining a tenuous hold there.

Rainwater flowing downhill over these slopes is an especially important erosional process in arid regions because vegetative cover is sparse. There are few roots to hold the soil, few plant structures to break the impact of falling raindrops and little soil humus to hold the moisture. A pelting rainstorm can cause extensive sheetwash in areas where the abundance of clay in the soil limits the infiltration of water. On steep slopes this thin, wetted layer can begin flowing downhill, unimpeded by vegetation, producing a mudflow. These examples serve to illustrate the paradox that erosion can proceed more rapidly in arid regions than in areas with abundant precipitation.

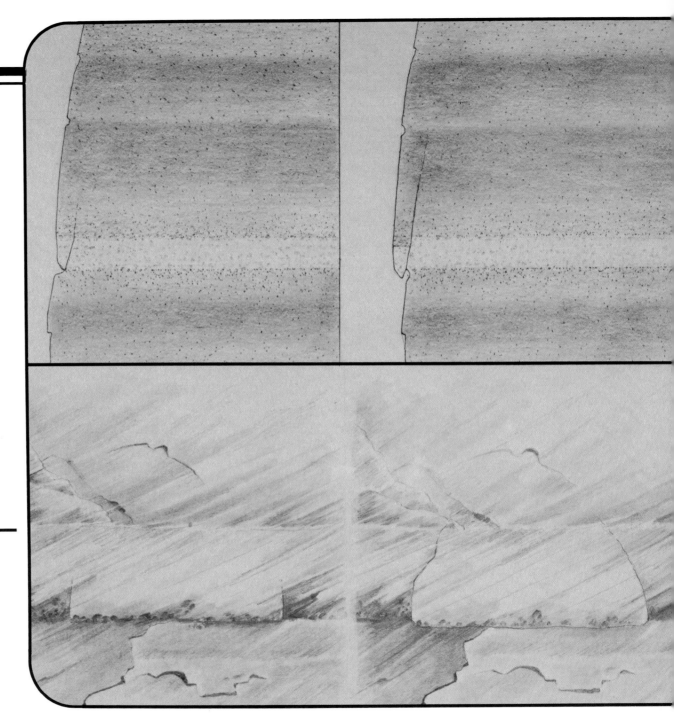

Fig. 34

The drawing represents side and frontal views of stages in the formation of an arch on a vertical cliff face. From left to right, preferential erosion produces a horizontal cleft in the rock face. This is frequently due to accelerated weathering along a spring line, sometimes the crumbling-away of sand grains in a coarse-grained layer. As the process proceeds, a portion of the cliff face becomes unsupported from beneath. As the slab hangs in tension, a fracture develops behind it, parallel to the cliff face. Expansion and contraction caused by heating and cooling may speed the development of the crack. When the mass of the free slab exceeds the shear and tensile strength of the rock, side fractures form, and the slab falls.

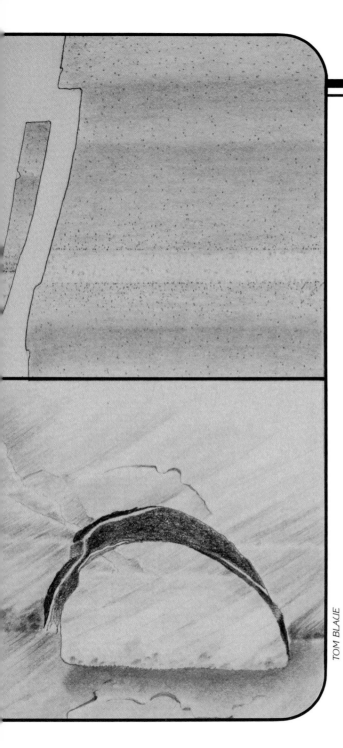

TOM BLAKE

Arch Formation

As you stand at the base of a precipitous cliff of Navajo Sandstone, perhaps at Upper Emerald Pool or at the foot of Cable Mountain, you will probably come to realize that the rock at the base of the cliff supports the great mass that lies above. The pressure exerted on the lower layer may exceed a million kilograms per square meter (about 1,000 tons per square yard). The sandstone is strong, but here and there throughout its thickness are weak zones consisting of coarse grained sand layers or silt bands. The former are readily transformed into shallow horizontal grooves on the rock surface by the decementing action of rainwater and subsequent crumbling of the rock. The latter are relatively impermeable to water flowing within the sandstone, so they serve to intercept the internal downward flow, bringing it to the surface as a seep or spring line. There the water weathers the clay siltstone stratum, causing a shallow recess.

Undercuts leave a portion of the cliff face unsupported, and the massive overhang of sandstone sags under its own weight. In time, the face will sag to the point where fractures develop. If there exists a joint behind the face and parallel to it, as is so often the case, the process goes even more rapidly to completion, and the great flake of sandstone comes crashing down to form a pile of rubble on the talus slope below, leaving an arch shaped recess in the face. Investigations at the Zion-Mt. Carmel Tunnel have provided evidence that thermal expansion and contraction may accelerate the process of arch formation.

The beauty of an arch is due to the graceful curvature at the top. As the overhanging slab sags prior to falling, the upper part of the slab undergoes enormous tensile stress while the rock is being pulled apart. This requires that millions of internal bonds in the cemented sandstone have to be broken as the developing fractures work their way upward. In nature, as in our lives, work is done in such a way that the least amount of effort is expended to get the job done. Clearly, a curved fracture will necessitate the breaking of the least number of bonds, about 20 percent fewer than in the case of a rectangular "arch". This conservation of work concept can be applied in many different geological situations.

The spalling of rock slabs from a cliff, bank erosion by a meandering river and the slumping of blocks of the rimrock are some of the most important mechanisms of canyon widening occurring today in Zion. The observation that the canyons are wider farther downstream suggests that the canyon widening process has been operating for a longer time there. This is entirely compatible with the fact that canyons extend themselves in an upstream direction, cutting farther and farther headward into the elevated plateau while deepening and widening. At the present time, deepening is occurring most rapidly in the steeper-gradient sectors, well upstream, while widening is most effective downstream in the sector where downcutting has exposed the softer underlying rocks. In the next chapter some fascinating developments in canyon evolution will be described, leading to some ideas as to the age of these canyons.

The canyon of the Right Fork
of North Creek as seen from
the West Rim Trail.

EVOLUTION OF THE CANYONS 2

Hundreds of thousands of us visit Zion. We come to find something; a little peace and quiet, a few lungfuls of clean air, incomparable vistas of color and immensity, and sometimes we also succeed in gaining a better understanding of the profound natural laws that are the basis of Zion and also our lives. Zion accepts us all, without complaint, and at times it seems that the deer find the added tolerance, the grasses muster up that extra resilience, the walls of crumbling stone resolve to stay their fall a bit longer. Moreover, we are welcomed by a ranger who seems capable of keeping us **and** the Park in good shape during our visit. But this is only an illusion, for Zion is real, and just as we are vulnerable when hiking the Narrows, Zion is very much susceptible to our presence.

Origin of the Existing Canyon Network

The present pattern of canyons formed by stream flow in Zion is due primarily to the presence of a pervasive and intricate array of joints and faults within the thick Navajo Sandstone. The streams have tended to follow these vertical planes of weakness, where it is easiest to cut downward. A. J. Eardley's map of joint systems in the Navajo Sandstone (Figure 35) very readily explains most of the present drainage network in the Park, especially that which is developed on the Navajo. At lower elevations where canyon-cutting has removed most of the Navajo (hence no joints are plotted on the map), the rectilinear alignment of canyons gives way to a more freely meandering configuration because the streams tend to erode these softer rocks almost without regard to the orientation of joints.*

Zion Canyon follows a boomerang-shaped joint (and fault?) system, very much like the one immediately to the west which runs from Wildcat Canyon through the Phantom Valley area. Parunuweap Canyon has developed within a dense set of shear joints formed by faulting with gentle monoclinal folding.** The Left and Right Forks of North Creek follow breaks which are now so completely erased by erosion of the Navajo that it is not clear whether they were joint sets or fault zones. Only a few parallel joint sets remain as evidence, high on the walls of these canyons.

The finger canyons in the Taylor Creek area are probably developed along tear faults formed during an interval of compression and folding. Hop Valley, Lee Valley and Trail Canyon are formed along the trace of the Cougar Mountain Fault. Almost everywhere within the Park it is possible to find canyons following zones of weakness developed in the Navajo as a result of complex but subtle deformation. (The origin of the joints and faults will be discussed in some detail in Chapter IV.)

There are a few canyons, however, that are exceptions to this rule. They do not seem to align with joint sets or fault zones. These are exemplified by Orderville and Echo Canyons and the upland canyon of Clear Creek along which runs the East Entrance road. I believe that these may be remnants of consequent drainages, that is, canyons developed in valleys which were originally occupied by streams flowing toward the northeast. These earlier stream valleys were a conse-

---

*Joints *are* present in the rocks underlying the Navajo; however they are generally more numerous, and the rocks are easily eroded in any case.

**On the south side of Parunuweap Canyon, the Springdale member of the Moenave Formation is higher than on the north side, indicating some offset or warping.

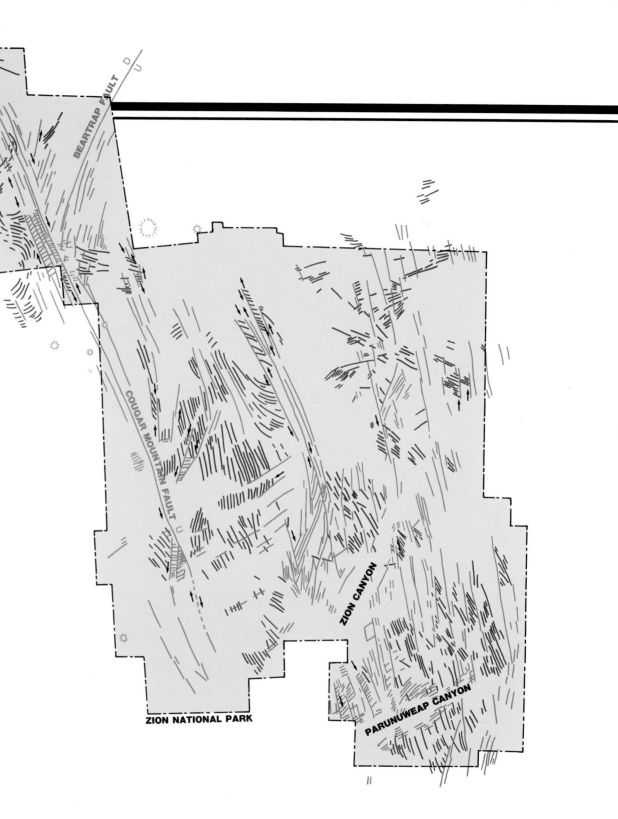

Canyons like these form on planes of weakness caused by jointing on a north-south axis.

Fig. 35

Joint systems in the Navajo Sandstone as recognized on aerial photographs and compiled on photo index sheets by A. J. Eardley in 1965. The Basin and Range Orogeny was a period of stretching–and the Sevier Orogeny a period of squeezing–of the continental crust in the southwestern United States. Boundaries are distorted because of distortions on the photo index sheets.

Joint System in the Navajo Sandstone of Zion National Park

RED—Joint set regarded as related to Basin and Range orogeny

BROWN—Joint set or sets regarded as **older** than Basin and Range orogeny

—Recent basalt cinder cones

APPROXIMATE POSITION OF HURRICANE FAULT

BEARTRAP FAULT

COUGAR MOUNTAIN FAULT

ZION CANYON

PARUNUWEAP CANYON

ZION NATIONAL PARK

quence of the tipping of the Markagunt Plateau toward the northeast during the past several million years. Bit by bit the movements on the Hurricane and Sevier faults tilted the almost flat-lying sedimentary rocks of this area so that they are now dipping in a generally northeast direction at an angle of roughly five degrees on average. The streams then probably flowed down the gentle dip slope in much the same way as do those north of Navajo Lake. It is likely that these drainage patterns were dendritic, shaped like the vein pattern of a leaf, rather than highly parallel or rectilinear, because the Cretaceous and Tertiary rocks on which they developed were relatively soft and easily eroded without regard to any jointing that may have been present. Moreover, these streams would not have carved deep canyons because they flowed over a gently sloping surface, feeding into a major stream that flowed along the escarpment of the Sevier Fault; probably first along the Sevier River, then perhaps through the areas now occupied by Coral Pink Sand Dunes State Reserve and Pipe Spring National Monument.

How is it then that this system of east flowing streams in gentle valleys has been replaced by deep canyons, draining to the south and west?

Fig. 36 A

Cross-sectional view across the Markagunt Plateau looking northward. Displacement on the Hurricane Fault (left side of the drawing) and Sevier Fault (right) has produced prominent fault scarps into which gullies are cutting by headward erosion of small streams. Streams on the fault block drain toward the southeast.

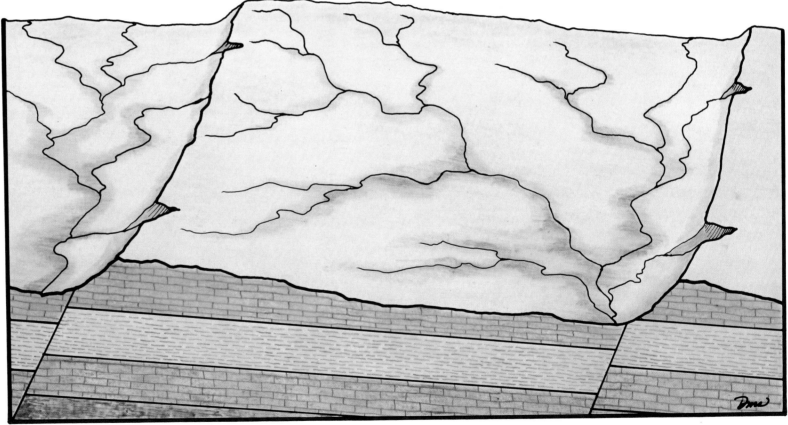

The western edge of the Markagunt Plateau has been elevated in stages by about 1,200 to 1,500 meters (4,000 to 5,000 feet) relative to the surface immediately to the west (Hurricane, La Verkin and St. George), according to Kurie (1966). That escarpment, abrupt as it was, was highly susceptible to erosion, and steep gullies must have developed rapidly on the western edge of the plateau, cutting headward toward the east.

The direction of headward cutting of these scarp canyons probably came early under the influence of zones of weakness within the dominant resistant stratum, the Navajo Sandstone. As these fast growing joint and fault controlled canyons worked their way farther and farther into the plateau, they intercepted more and more of the terrain drained by the consequent system of streams, pirating those headwaters and thereby gaining watershed and cutting power. Moveover, the pattern of groundwater flow, originally moving down the dip to the advantage of the consequent streams, was now reversed where the Navajo was being exposed, so that springs feeding the new canyon streams lowered the water table beneath the headwaters of the eastward flowing streams, robbing them of that source of water.

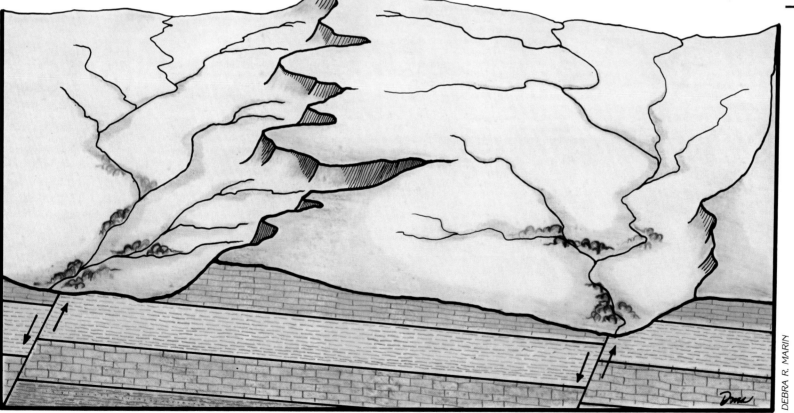

— *Fig. 36 B*

After millions of years, headward erosion by streams has produced great canyons, and the fault scarps have receded many miles to the east of the faults which started them.

DEBRA R. MARIN

Fig. 37

An aerial view of Firepit Knoll, a cinder cone at the head of Lee Valley. A depression is still clearly visible at the top. Navajo Sandstone cliffs tower in the background.

Fig. 38

Basalt flows in the Left Fork of North Creek. Beginning approximately a quarter-million years ago, some sixteen flows of lava cascaded into the canyon of the Left Fork, pouring from fissures in Cave Valley. The flows are now seen in cross section because the stream has reincised itself along the margin of the flow sequence.

CHARLES H. McCURDY

How Old Are the Canyons?

Zion's canyons are cut into sedimentary rocks of mid-Permian to late Cretaceous age, that is rocks dating from 240 to 80 million years ago, so the canyons are certainly much younger than that. The canyon-cutting period was probably initiated by the tilting of the Markagunt Plateau, caused by displacement on the Hurricane and Sevier fault systems, but that deformation event has not been dated any more accurately than "late Cenozoic" (Kurie, 1966). That would make the canyons less than about 15 million years old.

Clearly, what is needed in order to date these canyons are dateable layers deposited in one of the canyons; a deposit that has been cut through by subsequent erosion so that parts of it have been left attached to the canyon wall some distance above present stream grade. Then if we

were to measure the vertical distance up from the stream to the top of the dated deposit, we would know how long it took the stream to cut down to its present depth. This rate of downcutting could be used to calculate the age of the canyon.

Dating Volcanic Rocks

One has only to go to Lava Point to see that there are many such deposits in the Park. During the past 2 million years or so numerous volcanic eruptions have filled some of the developing canyons in Zion with lava flows, temporarily halting erosional activity. Crater Hill west of Coalpits Wash, and Spendlove Knoll and Firepit Knoll at the head of Lee Valley are young cinder cones marking the last episodes of volcanic action in Zion. These and many other associated volcanic vents (including Home Valley Knoll, a mile and a half west of Lava Point outside the Park) were the source of the black volcanic rocks that still cover much of the central and southwestern parts of the Park.

Moreover, as shown by the illustration of the North Creek flows (Figure 38), some of the lava-filled, deep canyons have been subsequently reincised and cutting has continued below the base of the volcanic flows.

Volcanic rocks can be dated by the potassium-argon (K-A) method, and because some of these flows have been dated, I will briefly describe how it is done. Basalt, the dominant volcanic rock here, contains among other trace constituents small quantities of the radioactive isotope potassium-40 (40 is the atomic weight). Slowly, but constantly, potassium-40 decays (disintegrates)

Fig. 39
Columnar jointing produced as the North Creek flows cooled is now exposed in the canyon south of Tabernacle Dome.

and changes into another element, argon-40, which is a non-radioactive gas. The rate of decay of potassium-40 is rather accurately known, and its half-life is about 1.9×10^9 years (that is, half the potassium-40 atoms in the rock will disintegrate in about 1.9 billion years creating an equal number of argon-40 atoms).

When lava flows out onto the ground, it is so hot that any gases it might contain, like argon-40, are lost. When it cools and solidifies, it contains very little, if any, argon-40. Yet when old samples of basalt are chemically analysed, traces of argon-40 are found. By shrewd geochemical analysis, it has been shown that the rock can be dated by measuring the amount of remaining potassium-40 and the amount of "new" argon-40 in a sample and making a calculation involving the half-life. Of course, the method is not as simple as described. It is a problem if the rock absorbs argon from the atmosphere or if the rock leaks

some of the argon-40 to the atmosphere. In spite of these and other problems, the K-A method is a reliable one, provided that the rock is not too young.

Unfortunately, much of the basalt in Zion *is* too young for traditional K-A dating. The only useful dates so far forthcoming on volcanic rocks in the Park have been those determined on older flows by Myron Best of Brigham Young University and Terrie Winnett at The Ohio State University. Best (personal communication), with the cooperation of Kenneth Hamblin, has provided dates for basalt from Lava Point and from a flow remnant atop a small unnamed mesa two miles north-northwest of Pocket Mesa, near the Kolob Terrace Road. They are 0.7 ± 0.2 million years (m.y.) for Lava Point and 1.40 ± 0.06 m.y. for the flow remnant. Best has also provided a useful date for the flow at the top of "Black Mesa", outside the Park about three miles west of Crater Hill.

The date is 1.00 ± 0.05 m.y. Best's other samples, of Crater Hill and North Creek flows, were apparently too young to be reliably dated.

More recent analyses by Winnett taking advantage of new techniques, have provided dates on younger flows. The oldest flow from Cave Valley (at Grapevine Spring in the Canyon of the Left Fork of North Creek) dates from about 0.26 m.y. An older flow from Crater Hill dates about 0.5 m.y., and the flow at the head of Lee Valley is approximately 0.7 m.y. old.

By making some reasonable assumptions, it is possible to calculate rates of canyon deepening in drainages adjacent to the dated flows. The flows occupied what were originally canyon and valley floors. In two of the cases subsequent erosion has taken place on both sides of the flow; so to determine the amount of continued downcutting since the flow, we must measure the amount of canyon development on both sides of the "inverted valley".

The values in the Table at right can be compared with rates (in meters and feet per thousand years) of *regional* downcutting (which should be less) for the area: for the Colorado River watershed, 0.16 m (0.54 feet) (Judson and Ritter, 1964); 0.43 m (1.4 feet) at Cedar Breaks (Eardley, 1966); 0.09 m (0.3 feet) for the Virgin River at St. George (Hamblin et al., 1975); and 0.24 m (0.8 feet) for the watershed of the South Fork of Taylor Creek (this work). They compare very well with a downcutting rate of 0.52 m (1.7 feet) per thousand years at the Hurricane Fault scarp at La Verkin (Hamblin et al., 1975).

Reference to the geological map shows that the different rates calculated here reflect downcutting through various rock types under diverse conditions of stream gradient (and discharge, it should be noted). The North Creek value represents erosion of soft rocks with a moderate stream discharge on a moderately steep gradient. The Kolob Creek and Blue Creek values are for downcutting of limestone terrain with small stream discharge and a steep gradient. The Pine Spring Wash and "Black Canyon" values are for a steep to gentle gradient over terrain which is partly Navajo Sandstone and partly mantled with basalt. Discharge there is very small.

Let us think of applying these calculated rates to solving the age of Zion Canyon at the Temple of Sinawava. First we must realize that in the past, when the Virgin River was just beginning to entrench its way into the top of the Navajo Sandstone at the Temple of Sinawava, discharge was much less than it is today. That watershed had not yet developed to its present extent. Moreover, we can think of the gradient as steep, perhaps like that in Blue Creek or Pine Spring Wash today. As time passed the discharge increased and the gradient decreased as the river cut deeper into the sandstone. Recently it has been cutting in soft Kayenta sediments at the Temple of Sinawava, so its downcutting is probably similar to that occurring in North Creek, where the gradient is steeper but the discharge is less.*

One weakness of the calculated rates is that

they are for V-shaped canyons, not for vertical-walled slots. The latter type of canyon-cutting proceeds much more rapidly, as can be seen by the abrupt deepening of the slot as one proceeds downstream into the Navajo Sandstone in upper Kolob Creek Canyon.

In spite of this, and other weaknesses, it is now reasonable to make a rough estimate of the age of the canyon at the Temple of Sinawava. The upper part of the canyon there is broadly V-shaped, through about 370 m (1,200 feet) of Temple Cap and Navajo Sandstone. The lower slot portion is about 340 m (1,100 feet) deep. Using the calculated values for steep terrain gives values of from 0.5 to about 1.9 million years for the time required to cut the upper part of the canyon.

The lower slot may have been cut more rapidly, in spite of the lower gradient, and an estimate for the length of time required to cut the lower 340 m might range from 0.2 to 1.8 m.y. depending on whether or not one uses faster or slower rates. Thus, a calculated age of the canyon at the Temple of Sinawava might lie between 0.7 and almost 4 million years; possibly closer to the latter figure.

The Temple of Sinawava lies about 32 km (20 miles) by river from the Hurricane Fault escarpment and about 16 km (10 miles) from the upper end of the canyon, where the river first encounters the Navajo Sandstone. If the age of the canyon is taken as zero at the upper end, then it can be argued (everything else being equal)

Rates of Erosion Near Dated Flows

Canyon	Amount of downcutting since flow		Rate of downcutting (Meters and feet per thousand years)	
	(Meters)	(Feet)	(Meters)	(Feet)
North Creek at Virgin Oil Field, below "Black Mesa"	210	700	0.22	0.72
Kolob Creek north of Lava Point	300	990	0.43	1.40
Blue Creek south of Lava Point	200	650	0.28	0.93
Pine Spring Wash west of unnamed mesa	390	1,290	0.28	0.92
"Black Canyon" one mile northwest of Pocket Mesa	130	440	0.09	0.31

*Presently the river is cutting recent alluvial deposits in Zion Canyon, and Pleistocene gravels are exposed at river level at Grafton.

an intermediate stage of development. The flows along Deep Creek a few kilometers north of the Park may be looked at for this purpose.

Parunuweap Canyon, the canyon of the East Fork of the Virgin, is thought to be younger than the canyon of the North Fork. The existence of waterfalls and a very steep gradient in the upper part of Parunuweap Canyon indicate that the slot is still being rapidly formed there.

Ancient Rockslides

Other deposits besides volcanic rocks have been left "high and dry" on the walls of the canyons. These record other events in the evolution of this terrain and, from the Visitor Center and the campgrounds, some can be seen forming tan to pink benches on the sloping valley walls. Visitors fortunate enough to be here when these deposits are formed will see the dust cloud and hear the rumble associated with rocks falling from the canyon walls.

These benches consist of calcium carbonate-cemented rock debris that has accumulated on the slopes beneath the towering Navajo Sandstone cliffs. Several bench remnants can be seen about 180 m (600 feet) above the Springdale Sandstone ledge beneath The Watchman and Bridge Mountain. Another caps the mesa immediately southwest of the Visitor Center. Similar benches can be found in the wider downstream sections of other canyons in the Park.

The rubble cap southwest of the Visitor Center contains enormous slabs of Navajo Sandstone oriented in such a way as to suggest that the broken mass slid to its present location from

V. L. JACKSON

Fig. 41
A Pleistocene talus deposit, cemented rock debris, forms a resistant bench, or ledge, visible to the southwest of the Visitor Center.

that the canyon has moved headward about 16 km (10 miles) in the past 0.7 to 4 million years. This would mean that the incipient Virgin River may have begun cutting into the edge of the fault escarpment near Hurricane about two to twelve million years ago.

All of these figures must be viewed with skepticism until other dates are available for flows that are more intimately associated with canyons in

The effects of a giant rockslide during July, 1983, are evident in these before-and-after photos of Timber Top Mountain.

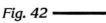
Fig. 42

Cross section across lower Zion Canyon between Mt. Kinesava and Johnson Mountain. Rockfall and slide debris have produced a large talus apron at the base of Mt. Kinesava that is moving slowly toward the valley floor. A smaller talus bench appears at the base of Johnson Mountain. The gentle dip of the bedrock toward the east promotes mass wasting and slump on the east-facing slopes. This explains why the Mt. Kinesava talus apron is larger than those on the east side of the canyon. "Qs" is Quaternary slide deposits and "s" and "al" are slide deposits and alluvium. The other formation name symbols are the same as given in Figure 2.

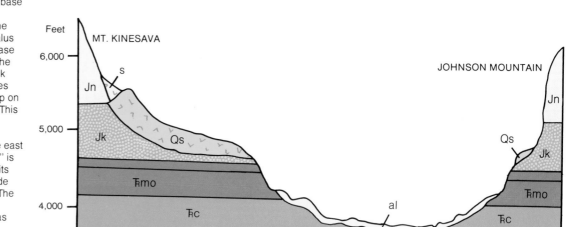

a source near the Meridian Tower. If so, this must have happened before Oak Creek Canyon was formed, in which case the cemented rubble aprons must be quite old.

Water from rain and snowmelt can flow easily through the very permeable broken rock debris and in so doing the slightly acid water dissolves calcite from the fractured sandstone. The water flows downslope through the rubble and seeps into the smaller pores. Eventually the pore water evaporates in this dry climate and a precipitate of calcium carbonate is left behind which, after many wet-dry cycles, cements the rubble. The cementation seems to indicate the antiquity of these deposits, as well as helping to preserve them.

The cementation of rock rubble aprons serves as an example of the way in which agricultural lands in arid regions can be ruined if too much calcite, salt or alkali accumulates in the soil. That is why local farmers irrigate by occasionally flooding the fields, to flush away accumulated evaporation products.

One of these talus aprons, at the base of Mt. Kinesava, seems to have behaved like a glacier. Figure 42 shows how a gap, like a crevasse, has formed between the talus and the base of the Navajo cliff, indicating that the slab of rubble is slowly moving down the slope.

So far, no way has been found to date the perched rubble aprons. If one day we are fortunate enough to find a piece of wood preserved where it was covered by rockfall, then radiocarbon dating may be possible.

Old Stream Deposits

The stream environment has left traces of its existence in the form of channel and floodplain deposits; the former being laid down on the bed of the stream and the latter being deposited only when the stream overflows its banks during floods. Such deposits have frequently been laid down by the Virgin River and other streams in the Park during the past, however only the more recent sediments have been preserved to any extent because erosion dominates over deposition in these canyons, and the fast-flowing streams tend to remove all traces of their earlier history (except for the "negative evidence" that is the canyon itself).

Exposures of stream deposits can be seen a few meters downstream from the powerlines that cross the river at the south end of Watchman Campground. Here and there over a distance of several hundred meters steep banks have been formed by the Virgin River as it now cuts laterally into its earlier deposits.* Where the banks are

Fig. 43
Pleistocene stream gravels exposed in Coalpits Wash. These firmly cemented gravels predate some Crater Hill volcanic activity. They were probably deposited during cooler, wetter times here.

Fig. 44
A reconstructed stream channel is shown superimposed over a cutbank exposing river and lake deposits near Birch Creek in Zion Canyon. This shows how terraces were formed in the past few thousand years by the Virgin River. The actual scene is shown in Figure 45.

steepest (being eroded most rapidly) on the out-side edge of meanders, multi-colored layers of clay, silt, sand and a few "lenses" of gravel have been exposed.

The coarser deposits of sand and gravel mark the location of earlier channels of the river, showing that the river has meandered as it cut downward. The clays and silts are the floodplain

---

*These river deposits are approximately 24 m (80 feet) thick in this area, as shown by the drilling log from the Springdale well on the floodplain opposite the Watchman Campground.

TOM BLAUE

Fig. 45

Stream terraces developed on river and lake deposits a short distance upstream from Birch Creek along the North Fork in Zion Canyon. Figure 44 shows how the Virgin River produced these terraces at an earlier time.

V. L. JACKSON

deposits of the river, laid down well above the river channel when the river swells and widens during floods.

The size of the sedimentary particles in the deposit is of principal importance in interpreting the depositional environment, because it tells us about the energy (velocity and turbulence) of the moving water. Because water turbulence is greater in the channel than on the floodplain, small particles of clay and silt do not remain long on the bed of the stream. Coarser materials like sand and gravel are the usual channel deposits.

Other good exposures of stream sediments can be seen about a hundred meters downstream from the Birch Creek footbridge on the west bank of the Virgin River. There, rounded boulder and cobble channel deposits overlie a chaotic mixture of silt, sand and large angular rock fragments. Rock fragments in the stream deposits have been smoothed and rounded by abrasion (and deposited in layers to some extent), but the underlying material was dumped there when a huge rockslide occurred. That slide and its effects are discussed in the next section.

Another good exposure can be seen at the first pulloff on the left, upcanyon from Birch Creek. If you walk to the stream bank, look across the river at the steep bank consisting of reddish floodplain silt overlying grayish channel gravels. The gravels overlie yellowish-gray clay, deposited in a lake which formed behind the slide mentioned above. Another interesting feature visible here is the terraced surface of the floodplain. There are two or three levels of valley floor separated by an elevation difference of only a few meters, representing successive stages in stream erosion. Figure 44 shows how this came about. The terraces are well developed here because downcutting was proceeding rapidly before construction of the concrete dam at Birch Creek.

Besides the important grain size characteristics, there are often other significant features to be seen in these sediments. They are structures that provide clues to the environment of deposition. If you walk over the floodplain near the stream, mudcracks may be seen provided you select a place where clay and fine silt have been deposited. Mudcracks are formed when floodwaters recede and the sun dries fine-grained sediment, forming roughly six-sided curly plates.

Stream deposits may also be characterized by a property called graded bedding. The term bedding refers to any number of essentially horizontal layers of sediment arranged one above the other, each bed being by definition more than 1 cm (0.4 inch) thick. Thinner layers are called laminae. The property of graded bedding means that the grain size of the sedimentary particles becomes smaller going from the bottom to the top of a bed.

Fig. 46
Modern mudcracks. The clay contracts into curly plates as it dries.

NATIONAL PARK SERVICE

There is much to be explored in understanding this statement. First, it is necessary to see that a sequence of sedimentary beds, or indeed the laminae that may make up each bed, represents a time sequence where the lower layers are older (were deposited earlier) than the upper ones. This characteristic of sediments is called rather portentously The Law of Superposition, and it enables one to read the history of sedimentation in a sequence of beds like the pages of a book. Graded bedding, therefore, means that over an interval of time the stream deposited successively smaller and smaller grains. This might record a time when over a few hours or days the discharge of the stream (its volume of flow) was decreasing, as it does after rainfall in the watershed. The competence of the water to remove large particles becomes less and less so that smaller and smaller ones could accumulate. Floodplain (and lake) deposits can be graded also. Turbid water standing quietly in large pools clears by dropping first the larger sand sizes, then silt, then clay.

Graded bedding can occur over a longer time interval in another way, and the pertinent principle is only a little more difficult to grasp. It occurs because streams (especially meandering streams) move laterally, sliding sideways over the centuries from valley wall to valley wall, and in this lateral translation the stream deposits finer material over coarser material. The turbulence of the current is greater on the convex side of the bend, hence only larger grains can accumulate there and the channel is deeper. Turbulence is least on the so-called point bar, on the concave side where the water is so calm that smaller sizes can accumulate. Here deposition is relatively rapid, and mud flats or sand bars can form.

Fig. 47

Fossil mudcracks from the Dinosaur Canyon member of the Moenave Formation provide evidence of stream flood deposits drying in the sun.

Fig. 48

Pleistocene stream-deposited sand, consisting of volcanic sand and cinders, showing tabular-planar cross-bedding in the lower half and a trough set in the upper left. The deposit is located south-southwest of Tabernacle Dome, at the point where hikers begin their descent into the Left Fork of North Creek.

When a stream erodes its banks, it does so mainly on the convex side, so that as the channel progresses sideways and downstream through the years, the point bar environment moves to the location previously occupied by fast-moving water. This is why coarser sediments are overlain by finer ones in this situation. The concept of moving environments of deposition is a handy one, and will be useful in discussions to follow in this chapter.

Non-horizontal bedding is called cross-stratification*, and channel deposits are especially well characterized by trough cross-stratification. As suggested by Figures 48 and 49, so-called trough sets are formed when trough-shaped furrows are cut into the streambed deposits by strong eddies or currents on the stream bottom and are subsequently filled in with sediment. Such currents often move about over the streambed, so that troughs are repeatedly formed and filled, leading to interlacing arrays of trough sets. A stream carrying an abundant load of sediment will deposit that sediment in its own path, so that the channel is forced to relocate, often on the adjacent floodplain.

The ripple marks (actually tiny dune structures) formed by fast-moving streams produce parallel ripple marks, but these may also be formed in sand by wind and are not necessarily diagnostic of stream environments. Water oscillating under the influence of waves in pools produces oscillation ripple marks.

---

*It is also frequently called cross-bedding, and I shall generally use this term for brevity here.

Fig. 49

Exposed cross section of a stream channel in the Moenave Formation on the switchbacks. Halfway up the exposure a stream current has cut a trough into the flat-bedded sediments. The trough was subsequently filled as stream turbulence declined or the main current moved to another location on the streambed.

Fig. 50 (inset)

Ripple marks in stream-laid sandstone of the Moenkopi Formation, in Scoggins Wash.

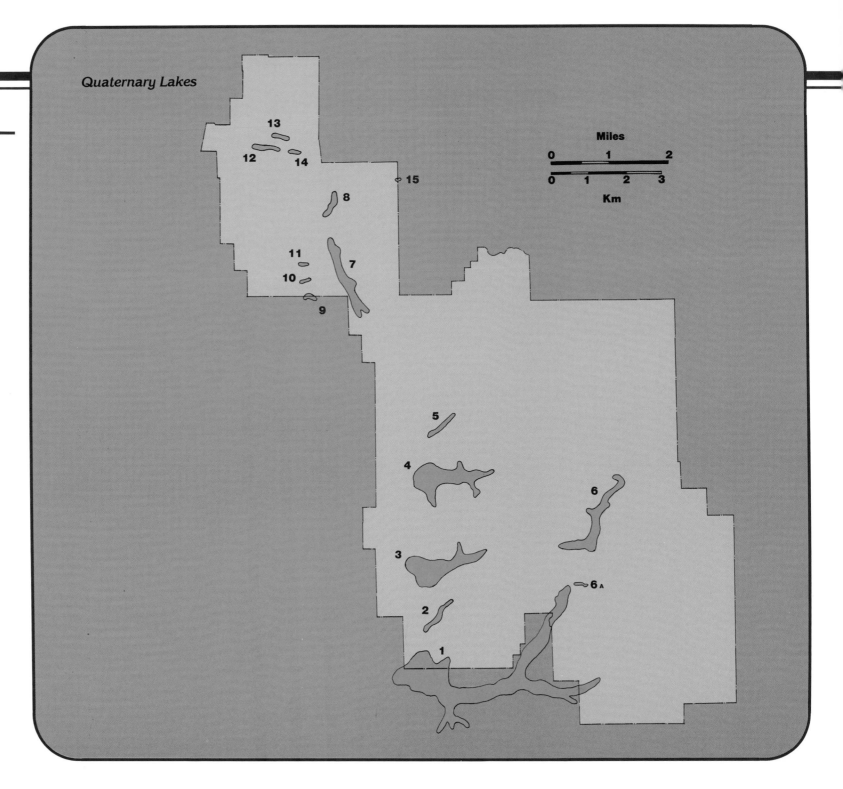

Fig. 51

Quaternary-age lakes in Zion National Park. Those of Pleistocene age were all lava-dammed, with one possible exception. They are: 1) Lake Grafton, 2) Scoggins Lake, 3) Coalpits Lake, 4) Trail Canyon Lake (slide-dammed in a later stage), and 5) Lake Fontelicella. Holocene lakes were dammed by slumps or slides and include: 6) Sentinel Lake (and nearby 6a. Pine Creek Lake), 7) Hop Valley Lake, 8) LaVerkin Creek Lake, 9) Smith Creek Lake, 10) Cane Creek Lake, 11) Currant Creek Lake, 12) Paria Lake, and 13) Middle Fork Lake. Existing slide-dammed lakes include: 14) Beatty Lake (seasonal) and 15) Potamogeton (Chasm) Lake.

Quaternary Lakes

Miles

Km

Quaternary Lakes

Zion National Park is located in a semiarid region which is undergoing rapid erosion, hence it may seem unlikely that major lakes have existed within these canyons in the past several hundred thousand years. There are however three lakes in the Park at this time. One, only a few years or decades old, is in Mystery Canyon, about 1.6 km (one mile) upcanyon from the Temple of Sina-wava. Another, Potamogeton (Chasm Lake), is nestled in a canyon east of Bullpen Mountain. The third existing lake, here called Beatty Lake, is near the mouth of the canyon of the South Fork of Taylor Creek. All these impounds are slide lakes, produced when rockfall blocked the respective canyons. They are each only a few hectares (1 acre = 0.405 hectares) in size, and except for Potamogeton Lake are quite likely to be dry during the summer months.

The deposits of much larger Holocene* lakes have been recognized by Grater (1945) and Eardley (1966). Moreover, the writer has located deposits of several other lakes, including two of Pleistocene** age. These deposits and the history they reveal are sufficiently interesting that I have described them in some detail here.

Hop Valley Lake

The youngest of the ancient lakes in Zion occupied Hop Valley, a lovely flat-bottomed canyon lying northwest of Spendlove Knoll vol-cano. The flat floor of Hop Valley is due to the thick accumulation of lake sediments there. Their

*The Holocene is the most recent 10,000 years of the Quaternary Period.
**The Pleistocene is the division of the Quaternary period dating from about 10,000 to about 1.6 million years ago.

—Fig. 52

Stump of a pine (probably ponderosa) in growth position, dating between 3,310 and 3,910 years before present. The living tree was inundated by Paria Lake, then buried by lake deposits. Recent erosion of the lake sediments by the South Fork of Taylor Creek has exhumed this and other trees in this drainage.

age is indicated by a radiocarbon date of 670 ± 200 years before present (b.p.) on wood taken from a layer 5 m (15 feet) below the uppermost lake sediments by Eardley (1966). The lake was formed when a large part of the ridge northeast of Burnt Mountain broke away along a joint system and blocked the north end of the valley. Eardley suggests that the rockslide dam may have formed about 1,500 years ago. The dam has only recently been breached, it appears, because only the top several feet of lake sediments have been removed by the stream there.

The slide material is as interesting as the lake deposits. You will notice on the topographic map of Zion that there is a large, nearly circular depression in the slide debris near the Hop Valley Trail. If you travel this area on foot you will find several such depressions, only the largest of which is shown on the 1979 topographic map. These depressions look like craters, not craters caused by any eruption of lava or steam, but depressions marking the violent eruption of compressed air trapped by the great mass of broken rock as it fell. The phenomenon of violent winds associated with rockfall was dramatically illustrated by the rockslide following the Hebgen Lake Earthquake in 1959 near Yellowstone National Park, Wyoming. Trees, cars and trailers were blown away from the nearby U. S. Forest Service Campground, and clothing was torn from people's bodies! This brings to mind the question whether or not the Hop Valley slide was caused by an earthquake, but there is simply no way of knowing.

At maximum extent Hop Valley Lake occupied an area of about 1.2 km² (0.46 square miles). Pieces of pine cones and bark embedded in sand can be seen in thin layers exposed on cutbanks in the south end of the valley providing testimony to ancient floods.

Paria Lake

This lake was formed when a small slide blocked the water gap formed by the Springdale Sandstone in the South Fork of Taylor Creek a few hundred meters downstream from the point where the Park road crosses that drainage. Roughly 9 m (30 feet) of sand, with some silt and thin clay bands, accumulated in this lake bed before the water overflowed the dam and breached it. Paria Lake occupied at most only about 0.1 km² (0.04 square mile).

The South Fork subsequently has cut completely through the lake deposits, exposing a complete cross section of lake history. Three pine tree stumps* have been exposed in this way at the base of the lake sediments. These trees were growing beside the stream bank when the lake formed, killing and covering them with sediment that has preserved them. One of the trees has been dated at 3,610 ± 300 years b.p., yet the wood is still quite sound today. The trees thus date the time of the slide there.

*Identification by Dendrochronology Laboratory, University of Arizona.

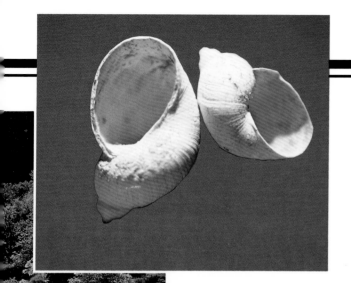

Fig. 53

Sedimentary evidence of Paria Lake. These thinly bedded sands and black organic layers probably mark the annual accretion of sediments on the bed of the lake. Except during brief wet periods of the year, the lake was probably more like a bog.

Fig. 54 (above)

Shells of *Succinea avara* from Paria Lake sediments, approximately 3X actual size. These snails live in damp areas near water and still occupy similar habitats in the Park. They are very widely distributed geographically, and the writer has seen identical shells in 8,500-year-old stream deposits in central Alaska.

Fig. 55 (above right)

Tan clay and red silt beds of Sentinel Lake exposed near the Lodge in Zion Canyon.

Eardley (1966) collected lignitic (blackened) wood about 3 m (10 feet) from the top of these lake sediments, which was dated at 2,880 ± 200 years b.p., so we know that this lake probably existed for several centuries. Pollen collected from these sediments by Hevly (1976) are similar to those produced today by vegetation growing in the area, so the climate (precipitation and temperature) was probably much the same then as now.

Snail shells found in the lake sediments indicate that the environment was more like that of a seasonal pond than a year-round lake. Terrestrial species included *Vallonia perspectiva* and *Discus cronkhitei. Succinea avara* was the only aquatic snail found, and it can survive prolonged periods of drought.

Sentinel Lake

As you drive the road between Canyon Junction and Birch Creek, going toward Zion Lodge, you will see contorted and broken beds of Kayenta sediments and slide debris forming the bench to the left, across the river. Some of this material is present on the right side as well. Only here and there does Springdale Sandstone bedrock peek through the mantle of superimposed rubble. This material is an enormous slump and slide block that moved away from the face of The Sentinel about 4,000 years ago and blocked the Virgin River, forming a lake over 1.8 km² (0.7 square miles) in area and extending upcanyon at least as far as the base of Angels Landing. According to Grater (1945) the slump was caused ". . . by an extensive fracture and joint system, water-saturated shale beds underlying the massive Navajo Sandstone, and a regional dip of 1° - 3° to the northeast."

A radiocarbon date of 3,600 ± 400 years b.p. on plant carbon in siltbands overlying thick gray lake clays in a dry fork of Birch Creek indicates the time when the dam was finally breached by the lake waters. The date of the slide has been calculated by measurement of presumed annual layers (varves) in the clays and by estimating the rate of transport of sediment by the river.

An excellent cross section of sediments deposited late in the life of the lake can be seen from the upper part of the Emerald Pools Trail near the river footbridge. The alternation of layers

EAST COUGAR MOUNTAIN FAULT

BLOCKED CANYON

SPRINGDALE CLIFF

SPRINGDALE CLIFF

REMNANT BASALT

of sand, silt, clay and gravel in that section indicates that the spillway was repeatedly blocked by slides for a time after breaching. In its earlier stages, the lake surface lay at least 15 m (50 feet) above Zion Lodge, but since the lodge is built upon nearly 100 m (300 feet) of lake deposits the water would have been at least 115 m (350 feet) deep during the early years in the life of the lake. Unlike other Quaternary lakes in Zion, Sentinel Lake was nearly full of water year-round.

Subsequent erosion by the river has cut through over half the thickness of the lake deposits, yet there is enough remaining to give Zion Canyon a flat bottomed aspect between Birch Creek and Weeping Rock.

Trail Canyon Lake

If you hike up the Right Fork of North Creek (located a few kilometers north of Coalpits Wash), you will see erosional remnants of basalt high up on the walls at the mouth of the canyon and about .4 km (¼ mile) farther upstream. These are outliers of the great mass of basalt that forms the northwest wall of North Creek below the confluence and up the Left Fork canyon as well; basalt that flowed into the canyons from volcanic vents located in upper Cave Valley, near Spendlove Knoll and Firepit Knoll volcanoes. About .4 km (¼ mile) farther upstream from the easternmost basalt you will see on the north side of the canyon a mass of slide material that towers several tens of meters (hundred feet) overhead. You may also notice that some of the slide debris fills an older, abandoned canyon of the Right Fork. The present canyon is located to the south of the blocked one and is formed in the Springdale Sandstone Member of the Moenave Formation. As you wind your way through this narrow canyon, you soon come out into the open again, where Trail Canyon enters from the south. At this point you are standing on the East Cougar Mountain Fault.

If you now look to the north and northeast you will see very light tan colored sand capping the bench about 60 m (200 feet) above stream level. Another .4 km (¼ mile) upstream you can turn left into a wash that takes you into an area where Trail Canyon Lake sediments are very well exposed. The upper 15 m (50 feet) of the sediments are dominated by sand, but thin layers of clay, with some limy deposits (called marl) dominate in the lower 30 m (100 feet) of section. There is one thin layer of limestone near the top of the section.

The evidence seems to indicate that this 2 km² (0.8 square mile) lake was formed behind a basalt dam. The elevation of the basalt outlier is the same as the elevation of the top of the sand-capped bench, suggesting that volcanic activity was the cause. It is also possible that the Right Fork was dammed by a slide which moved down from Cougar Mountain, because the lake sediments overlie slide material. I tend to think however that the slide occurred early in the life of Trail Canyon Lake, caused perhaps by the unstabilizing effect of an elevated water table which the high lake waters would have produced. Yet because there is some uncertainty about the correlation with the basalt, the age of the lake is open to question.

Hevly's analysis of pollen from Trail Canyon

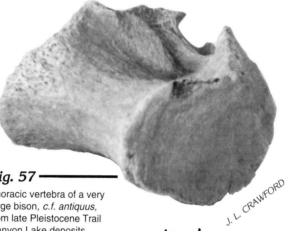

Fig. 57 ———

Thoracic vertebra of a very large bison, *c.f. antiquus,* from late Pleistocene Trail Canyon Lake deposits. Scale is 1 centimeter. Identified by James E. Martin, Museum of Geology, South Dakota School of Mines.

J. L. CRAWFORD

Lake clays turned up a higher proportion of ponderosa pollen than in any other samples so far examined. Yet ponderosa is relatively uncommon in that watershed today.

Trail Canyon Lake had a second, higher level, definitely caused by a slump from a mesa to the north. This slump material forms the high bench that towers over the debris-filled early canyon downstream. The higher bench is capped by only a few meters of tan sand, but the level surface of that sand cap indicates that the lake stood briefly at an elevation fully 180 m (600 feet) above the present canyon floor. When this high dam was breached, the torrential flow excavated a new canyon several hundred meters south of the original one. Again, this offset from the main lake basin is what has helped to preserve these ancient sediments for investigation today.

Snail shells have been found in clays and marls near the top of the lower lake sediments that are similar to those from Coalpits Lake. One species, *Planorbella tenuis,* had not been known previously in Zion.

A fossil thoracic vertebra of a large bison was found associated with gravels and a fish vertebra at the top of the lower bench. This also tends to support the idea of a Pleistocene age for the Trail Canyon Lake sediments.

Coalpits Lake

Around a half million years ago volcanic activity broke through the surface in the vicinity of Crater Hill, sending floods of steaming lava through the surrounding canyons and valleys. Coalpits Wash was blocked by one of these flows and a lake was formed. In its later stages Coalpits Lake may have occupied over 2.5 km² (one square mile) of area, but the sediments that remain show conclusively that it was usually a seasonal lake, often dry except after spring snowmelt or heavy rains.

The lower layers of the approximately 45 m (150 feet) of lake sediments record a series of volcanic eruptions that sent clouds of fine cinders flying into the lake. Then, for many years the volcano was quiet, and living things moved back into the area. Tracks of various insects and animals, including those of a large bird (perhaps a goose), and even a camel have been found in the thin limestones of the early lake deposits. The muds of the lake bottom supported a healthy fauna, including mollusks, as indicated by preserved burrows. Aquatic plants like *Potamogeton* (pondweed) have left clear impressions. Clays

Fig. 58

Tracks preserved in silty limestone deposits of Coalpits Lake, approximately 0.5 million years before present. *A)* Camel track. *B)* Bird track, possibly from a goose. *C)* Insect tracks. Upper trackway is that of an ant. Beetle tracks cross the middle of the photo. An aquatic insect larva trail makes a zig-zag in the lower left. The scale is 1 centimeter. *D)* Trackway of an unknown insect.

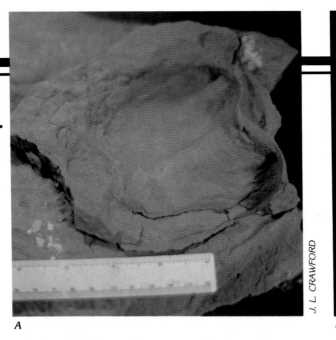

A

J. L. CRAWFORD

B

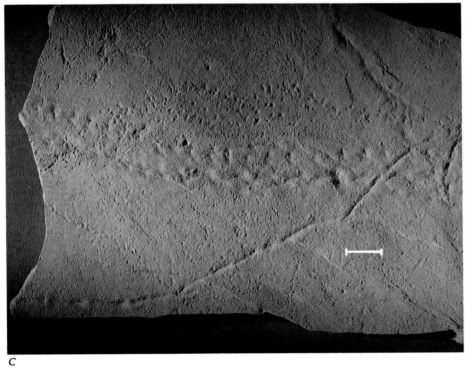

C

D

62

deposited later, after other eruptions of Crater Hill, contain abundant mollusks, especially *Gyraulus parvus,* an aquatic snail.

Eventually this lake also breached its dam, forming a new canyon at the east margin of the lava flows. Coalpits Lake probably existed for several centuries, but its sediments would probably have been entirely removed by erosion if not for the fact that its spillway developed well to the east of the main part of the lake basin.

Hevly's analysis of pollens in these lake clays shows that vegetation growing in the watershed at that time was much different from that growing there today. The pollen are dominated by trees like ponderosa and pinyon pine. Fully ten percent of the pollen is from spruce and fir trees. Yet today the Coalpits Wash area is the hottest and driest area of the Park. Only a few ponderosa and fir trees now grow in the very highest parts of the watershed and there are no spruce. The climate must have been considerably cooler and somewhat wetter then.

Other Lakes

Sediments of other Quaternary lakes have been seen near Burnt Mountain, but they have not yet been thoroughly investigated. There are probably other lake deposits in the Park that will be found in the future.

On the other hand, there have been lakes that have left little evidence of their existence. The largest of these was formed when the Virgin River was dammed by the Crater Hill flows. This lake, which I like to call Lake Grafton after the ghost town nearby, probably covered 26 km² (10 square miles) and extended upcanyon as far as the Visitor Center. Yet its life may have been so short that few true lake sediments were left or, if present, they may have been later reworked by the river. In any case, the thick accumulation of river deposits between the Visitor Center and Grafton is probably largely due to the ponding influence of that event.

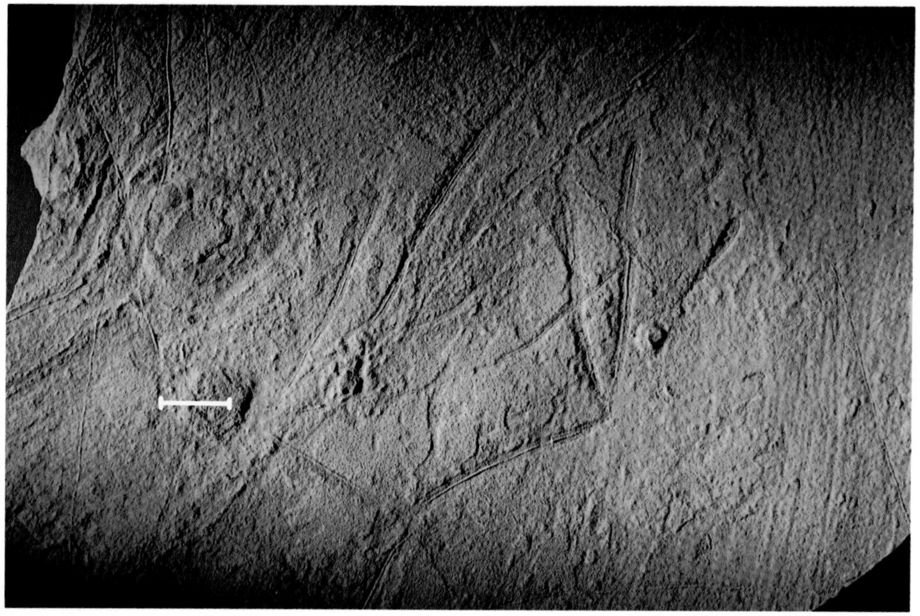

Geologic History: Left Fork of North Creek

The canyon of the Left Fork of North Creek is a little over 11 km (7 miles) in length and runs almost straight southwestward from its head near Corral Hollow on the west rim of the Horse Pasture Plateau.

Its history of development is of interest because a seemingly isolated population of rare snails has been newly discovered by malacologist Alice Lindahl at Grapevine Spring near the lower end of the canyon and about 1.1 km (0.7 miles) above the confluence with the Right Fork of North Creek (the former Great West Canyon). This interest arises because there are fundamental questions as to the mobility, adaptability and longevity of this and similar molluscan species. For the rest of us, it is perhaps more than a little surprising that an aquatic snail, a near relative of marine gastropods, and an animal which cannot survive when removed from the water, should be

Fig. 59

Fossil pondweed (*Potamogeton?*) in silty limestone of Coalpits Lake deposits. Scale is 1 centimeter.

able to persist at an isolated spring in an arid land far from the sea where the surface is being eroded at the rate of about 30 centimeters (1 foot) per thousand years.

The mollusk is tentatively named *Fontelicella*, and there are reasons to believe that it may be a new species (Lindahl, personal communication). The canyon where it lives has been developed in the Navajo, Kayenta, Moenave and Chinle formations of Jurassic and Triassic age. Chinle sediments are exposed only downstream from Grapevine Spring, and the Temple Cap and Carmel formations outcrop only in the highest parts of the watershed. Pleistocene basalts have played an important role in the evolution of the canyon and development of habitat for the *Fontelicella* population and are prominently exposed along the northwest wall of the lower 5 km (three miles) of the canyon. Grapevine Spring which provides the snails' habitat issues from the base of a sequence of basalt flows at the foot of Grapevine Wash, actually the lower end of Cave Valley.

The canyon of the Left Fork has been incised through about 820 m (2,700 feet) of sandstones, siltstones and mudstones (from the top of the Navajo to about halfway through the Moenave) in the vicinity of Grapevine Spring. Calculated rates of downcutting in similar terrain in Zion, based on potassium-argon dates of basalts, indicate that the Left Fork canyon is between about one and three million years old in that location.

Presently the discharge from the spring falls about 18 m (60 feet) into the channel, about one hundred meters away, by way of a small stream which flows over Moenave sandstone. Spring discharge was 0.028 CMS (1 cfs) in 1975. It issues from interflow clinker horizons and fractures at

and near the base of a 150 m (500 feet) thick sequence of basalt flows on the northwest wall of the canyon. The basalt was derived from volcanic vents in Cave Valley near the Spendlove Knoll cinder cone. Lava flowed down Cave Valley into the canyon of the Left Fork and moved downstream at least 5 km (3 miles) past the confluence with the Right Fork. Basalt outliers located a short distance upstream in the Right Fork canyon show that the flows blocked that canyon as well.

Winnett and Sutter (personal communication) have obtained a tentative potassium-argon date on the lowermost basalt flow at Grapevine Spring which tells us that the stream channel was flooded with lava at a temperature of roughly 1,000°C (1,800°F) to a depth of about 150 m (500 feet) approximately 0.26 m.y. ago. It is believed unlikely that living organisms could have survived, and of course Grapevine Spring (or equivalent) did not exist at that time because the basalt did not become an aquifer until long after it had cooled.

About 2.4 km (1.5 miles) upcanyon from Grapevine Spring other basalts appear to represent two separate flows predating the Cave Valley basalts, as indicated by the greater amount of erosion of the basalts at the foot of Lee Valley. The probable elevation of the canyon floor at the time of these flows (as indicated by flow bottom elevations) was about 170 m (550 feet) higher than at present. One of the older flows appears to have moved down Little Creek from the vicinity of Home Valley Knoll, and it may be related to the flows at Lava Point which Myron Best has dated at about 0.7 m.y. ago. It is assumed, but cannot be proved, that these older flows also blocked the Left Fork.

The following sequence of lava damming of the Left Fork Canyon is proposed. At about 0.7 m.y. a flow moved down Little Creek and into the Left Fork at the foot of Lee Valley, where it may have blocked the canyon. The top of the dam would have been at an elevation of about 1,680 to 1,740 m (5,500 to 5,700 feet). If a lake formed, it may have extended upcanyon as far as the base of North Guardian Angel. Then, perhaps a few tens of thousands of years later, another flow, from Lee Valley, cascaded into the Left Fork Canyon. If a dam formed, a lake similar to the one described above would have developed.

The field evidence certainly shows that about 260,000 years ago a lava dam was produced by the Cave Valley flows. With the dam top at an elevation of about 1,490 m (4,900 feet), the lake would have extended upcanyon more than 1.6 km (1 mile). For the purpose of this discussion it will be convenient to refer to it as Lake Fontelicella.

Studies of other Quaternary lakes in Zion suggest that they were probably never deep for extended periods of time. They were probably subject to great seasonal variations in level and were turbid during spring snowmelt and after summer thundershowers. It is believed likely that the lake water was highly alkaline, with the usual moderate stream water alkalinity augmented by dissolution of volcanic rocks. The water may have become relatively saline at times due to evaporation, particularly early in the life of a lake before it overflowed the dam.

Study of the sediments of Coalpits and Trail Canyon Lakes makes it possible to postulate a reasonable sequence of events in the Left Fork. The earlier lakes in the Left Fork Canyon pre-

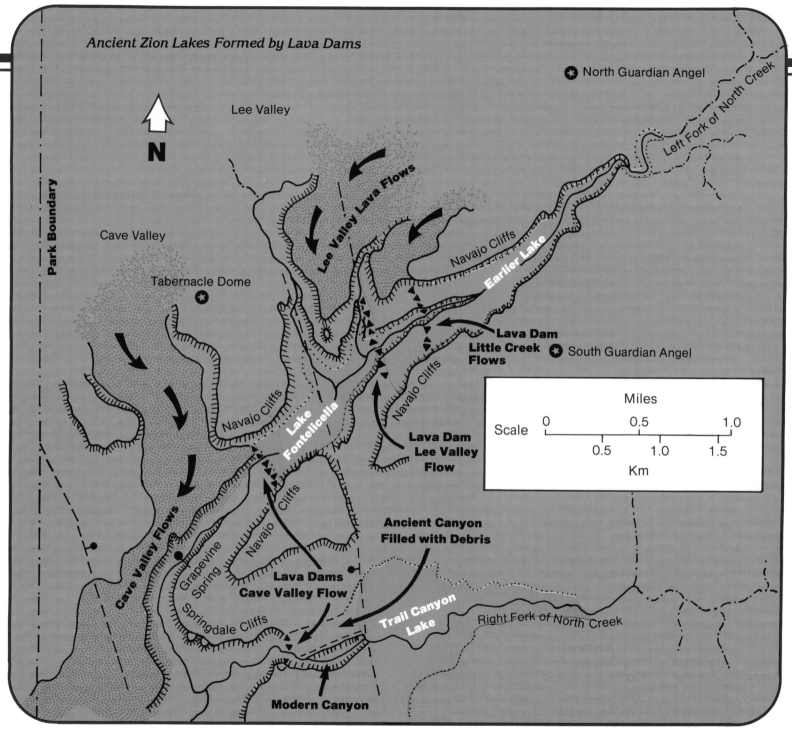

Ancient Zion Lakes Formed by Lava Dams

N

Park Boundary

Lee Valley

North Guardian Angel

Left Fork of North Creek

Cave Valley

Tabernacle Dome

Lee Valley Lava Flows

Navajo Cliffs

Earlier Lake

Lava Dam
Little Creek
Flows

South Guardian Angel

Navajo Cliffs

Lake
Fontelicella

Navajo Cliffs

Navajo Cliffs

Lava Dam
Lee Valley
Flow

Cave Valley Flows

Grapevine
Spring

Navajo
Cliffs

Lava Dams
Cave Valley Flow

Ancient Canyon
Filled with Debris

Springdale Cliffs

Trail Canyon
Lake

Right Fork of North Creek

Modern Canyon

Scale

Miles
0   0.5   1.0
0.5   1.0   1.5
Km

Fig. 60

Map showing the canyon of the Left Fork of North Creek, the lower portion of the canyon of the Right Fork, three important basalt flow sequences, the inferred locations of lava dams (now removed by erosion), and the approximate positions of shorelines of lakes which formed behind those dams. Trail Canyon Lake and Lake Fontelicella were probably contemporaneous, dating from approximately 0.26 million years before present. Two earlier lakes probably formed behind flows which blocked the Left Fork.

sumably caused by the Little Creek and Lee Valley flows, if they existed, would have had histories similar to that of Lake Fontelicella. Lake Fontelicella probably existed for several centuries with minimal overflow because the water could rise high enough to offset evaporation and seepage losses only after considerable sedimentary infilling of the basin. Only after this period of filling did the spillway begin to cut a channel, along the southeast side of the basalt that filled the Left Fork Canyon. It is difficult to estimate how long this cutting of a new canyon took in its various stages, but it is certain that the lava marginal canyon was developed in an upstream direction. Thus the canyon must have been quite deep in the vicinity of Grapevine Spring before the dam was breached and the lake drained.

Calcite-cemented clinker and flow breccia horizons at various levels above the canyon floor constitute evidence of a time series of earlier springs like Grapevine Spring at the lower end of Grapevine Wash. It appears that as the new canyon was being formed below Lake Fontelicella various springs, now dry, issued from the basalt. These were fed by lake water and Cave Valley groundwater finding its way through internal fractures and clinker layers in the basaltic dam. From a geologic standpoint, it would seem that suitable habitat for *Fontelicella* would have been available within the developing canyon downstream from, and contemporaneous with, the lake.

The present Grapevine Spring is only about 30,000 to 60,000 years old, based on calculated rates of downcutting. This age is the time at which the Left Fork had reached the base of the basalt while reincising its canyon. Yet as men-

The "Subway" is an unusual development of a slot canyon in the Left Fork of North Creek.

tioned there had been earlier springs at higher elevations nearby which had flowed from the basalt directly into the Left Fork, unlike the present situation where the spring discharges about 18 m (60 feet) above the bottom of the canyon.

The time interval between the times of presumed origin of the older lava-dammed lakes are roughly the same as the interval from the origin of Lake Fontelicella to the present. If *Fontelicella* at Grapevine Spring derived from a population in Lake Fontelicella, then it seems possible that some of the population could have survived from the earlier lakes as well.

As one begins to see the profound changes that have occurred in these canyons over the past thousands and tens of thousands of years, one tends to become more of a "realist". By that it is meant that one suddenly realizes the significance, for example, of that large boulder near the South Entrance Station. It wasn't always there was it? No, it came from up there on the Springdale ledge. And yes, it made a great crashing noise when it came down, probably splintering a few large trees as well on the way.

From this observation, one sees that every object has a history, whether it is a pebble in the river or a boulder at the base of a cliff. One realizes that these objects have a future as well, and one might not necessarily enjoy pondering such ideas while walking on a canyon trail as the setting sun casts its glow on the wall of rock that towers above.

One can be sure that it will be only a relatively short time before another great slide occurs, per-

Calcite-cemented basalt in the Left Fork of North Creek shows an earlier, higher location of Grapevine Spring. Water percolating through the permeable basalt deposited the calcite.

haps producing another lake in Zion Canyon. When and where no one can really say, but my guess puts Mt. Moroni near the top of the list. The Organ by Angels Landing is another likely candidate. Zion's canyons are still being formed, and we are merely witnesses.

MESOZOIC HISTORY 3

The more you look, the more you see.

R. M. PIRSIG

*Zen and the Art of
Motorcycle Maintenance*

By mid-Permian time Earth was already over four billion years old. The oceans and continents, though not in their familiar present configurations, had been in existence for almost three billion years, and many of the emigrant plants and animals had long since moved from the sea to colonize the continents. By 240 million years ago these had developed into widespread and diverse populations which covered the land.

A late Permian global map would show the great continent geologists call Pangaea in a vast ocean (Panthalassa) which occupied the rest of the Earth's surface. Pangaea began to split apart in late Permian time, breaking up gradually into the continents we now recognize. Before Pangaea there had been other continental configurations. For example, Europe and North America had come together in collision a few hundred million years earlier, the impact forming the Appalachian Mountains. But now, with the breakup of Pangaea, pieces began splitting off as perhaps never before, moving like slabs of ice on a windy pond to their present locations. And they are still moving.

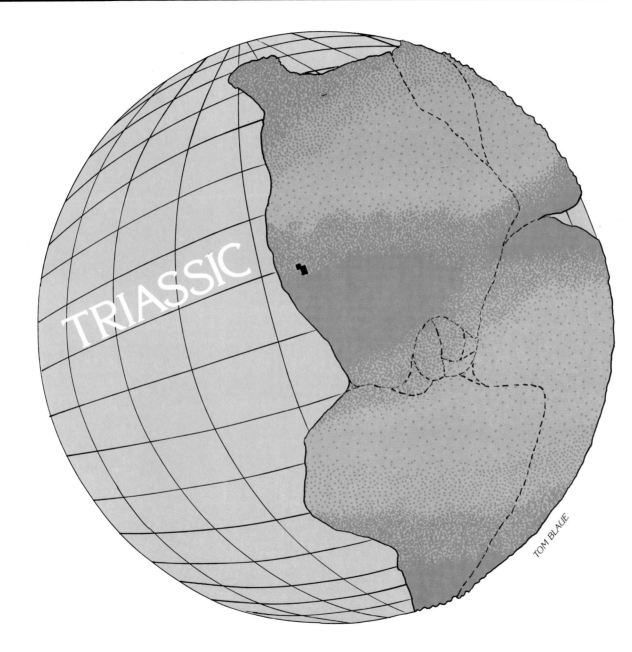

TRIASSIC

TOM BLAUE

Geologists see the crust of the Earth as consisting of a number of crustal plates "floating" on the mantle. The continents are viewed as thick, low-density parts of the crust (the ocean floor crust is denser and thinner). As the plates move, they may push against each other, pull apart or slide against each other. These compressive, extensional and shearing interactions shall be discussed in more detail later, but it is worth noting here that volcanoes, active faults and zones of major deformation of the crust, including growth of mountains, occur primarily along plate boundaries.

As we trace the history of Zion from mid-Permian to late Cretaceous time we shall be doing so by observing in the rocks evidence of past environments. The two aspects of environment that are most important and that leave their impression most clearly in the rock record are elevation and climate. Elevation means the altitude with respect to sea level. Certain kinds of sediments and fossils will be deposited in sea water (below sea level), others in the shore environment (at sea level), and distinctly different kinds inland (above sea level).

The imprint of climate upon sedimentary accumulation can be almost as distinct. The types of sediment and sedimentary structures that form in cool, moist climates are different from those that develop in warm, arid climates. The Arabian Desert and the Everglades are both near sea level and at about the same latitude; yet the land surface and the types of accumulating sediments and fossils are quite different because of the different climates.

And how does this tie in with moving crustal plates? Studies of magnetism locked into ancient rocks show that North America has moved northward and rotated counterclockwise since the breakup of Pangaea (see Figure 61). This has moved our area from the equatorial zone into the dry northern tropical zone. Along with these horizontal movements there have been both uplift and downwarp of the crust in this area, producing a range of terrestrial and marine environments with their respective sediments and fossils.

This dynamic history has been pieced together by geologists uncovering bits of evidence here and there in rocks from all over the Earth. It is a history that is only gradually emerging from patient, painstaking work and is only vaguely understood. There are many missing facts, many assumptions and worse, many contradictions. Still, let us look at the rocks here to see what they say about Zion.

Fig. 61

Schematic representation of the breakup of the supercontinent Pangaea between Triassic (left) and Cretaceous (right) times. Presumed subtropical desert areas are shown by the lighter stippling. As the North American continent moved northward, the Zion area was brought under the influence of different climatic zones, passing for a significant time through the latitudes where desert conditions predominate.

Kaibab Formation
(MIDDLE PERMIAN)

The Kaibab Formation outcrops within the Park only in two small areas in the northwest corner along the escarpment of the Hurricane Fault. The formation forms cliffs and is well exposed there, particularly near the Park. While it is the oldest (lowest) rock outcropping in Zion, it is essentially the youngest formation on the Kaibab Plateau to the south where it forms the upper rimrock at the Grand Canyon. The word Kaibab (Kaiba in the Paiute language) purportedly means reclining mountain.

Gregory's (1950) description of the Kaibab is, "White to yellowish massive, more or less dolomitic limestone, in part cherty, fossiliferous, locally gypsiferous." The presence of limestone containing dolomite, gypsum and characteristically marine fossils indicates that the Kaibab was formed near shore under warm and arid climatic conditions, sometimes under water depths of several meters, sometimes above sea level. Gypsum is a reaction product of anhydrite (calcium sulfate, $CaSO_4$) which forms when seawater evaporates in restricted embayments. As the seawater becomes increasingly saline with continued evaporation, anhydrite (not salt) begins to precipitate and accumulate as a white, muddy deposit. Dolomite ($MgCO_3$) is thought to be formed when hypersaline seawater reacts with the limy accumulation of calcium carbonate skeletal remains of marine organisms.

McKee (1952) lists brachiopods, bryozoans, corals, crinoids and sea urchins as major fossils in the Kaibab in this area. Near the top of the formation mollusks become predominant, indicating changing conditions as the sea withdrew and water became shallow. Preservation of fossils in Kaibab outcrops in and near the Park unfortunately is quite poor.

It is worthwhile to pause briefly to consider how limy mud becomes limestone. The mud consists of microscopic pieces of crystalline calcium carbonate secreted by marine organisms and parts of their skeletal structure. Because calcium carbonate is relatively soluble in water, the smaller microcrystals tend to dissolve while the larger ones tend to grow. In time the mud is converted to a three-dimensional array of relatively large interlocking calcite crystals held together in the same way as a jigsaw puzzle. Lithification (literally meaning turning to stone) of limy mud is thus similar to the conversion of powder snow into ice on polar glaciers where the temperature never reaches the melting point.

Figure 61 shows that in Kaibab time Zion was located at the western edge of Pangaea at a latitude of about 10° north of the equator. If Pangaean climatic belts were similar to those of today, then the climate of the Kaibab shore may have been like that of coastal Ghana (west Africa), a moderately dry equatorial land.

There is supporting evidence for this interpretation in the sedimentary structures of nearby strata. McKee and Oriel (1967) show that Permian wind direction in northern Arizona was northerly (from the north) based on analysis of cross-bed directions in windblown sand. This would place Zion in the northern hemisphere belt of tropical northeasterlies at that time, taking into account the counterclockwise rotation of North America since Permian time.

The Kaibab sea was a marine invasion of the continent, the largest of Permian time, and it was probably due to gentle subsidence of the crust in this area. More than 180 m (550 feet) of sediment were deposited before the sea began to withdraw (meaning that the crust ceased subsiding or was slowly elevated), placing the land increasingly under the influence of terrestrial conditions. An erosional surface of gentle relief marks the top of the Kaibab Formation, closing the Paleozoic Era in southwestern Utah in a very modest fashion. Time boundaries in geological history are seldom heralded by events on a world-wide scale.

J. L. CRAWFORD

Fig. 62

View north along the
Hurricane Fault near
Hurricane, Utah. Kaibab
limestone capped by basalt
can be seen on the east limb
of the Kanarra Fold.

Moenkopi Formation
(EARLY TRIASSIC)

The Mesozoic Era began in Zion much as the record of the Paleozoic Era ended, with a shallow sea occupying the western edge of the continent. Yet the fossils are quite different from those in the Kaibab Formation. They include marine pelecypods, snails and ammonites *(Meekoceras)*. The faunal change may have been due to changes in seawater chemistry or other wide-reaching influences. The earliest deposits of Triassic sediments here are assigned to the Moenkopi Formation which derives its name from Moenkopi Wash, where it is well exposed in northern Arizona.

Moenkopi rocks are well exposed also in the southwest and northwest corners of the Park. The formation changes in lithology from bottom to top in response to the gradual and vacillating withdrawal of that shallow sea, and it forms pink, white and chocolate-brown slopes, scantily covered by vegetation in this area. In Zion the formation is nearly 550 m (1,800 feet) thick and consists of shales, siltstones, sandstones, gypsum, mudstones and limestones, roughly in order of decreasing abundance.

The lower member of the formation, the Timpoweap Member, consists largely of brecciated (fragmented) limestone, indicating a history of cave collapse after considerable dissolution by fresh groundwater. This shows that the area was elevated above sea level after deposition of the limestone. The other members are the Lower Red, Virgin Limestone, Middle Red, Shnabkaib and Upper Red. The existence of fossil mud cracks, current ripple marks and thinly laminated bedding in the "red-bed" members higher in the section attest to a seasonal climate and slow moving streams on a broad, gently sloping coastal plain. Aridity alternating with occasional inundation by the sea are indicated by the gypsum and fossiliferous limestones. Fossils from the Virgin Limestone Member are illustrated in Figure 63.

The red coloration of the "red-bed" members of the Moenkopi (and higher formations) is due to finely disseminated hematite, frequently a characteristic feature of terrestrial sediments deposited under atmospheric conditions. The terrestrial aspect of the Moenkopi generally increases upward as the early Triassic sea gradually withdrew westward and Zion became more "continental".

An unconformity (erosion surface) of low relief truncates the top of the Moenkopi, marking an important interval of high energy erosion by streams. Thus there is no rock record here of mid-Triassic time.

— *Fig. 63*

Fossil "starfish" from the Virgin Limestone Member of the Moenkopi Formation. Collected near Virgin, Utah, by Margot Hamilton. Scale is 1 centimeter.

J. L. CRAWFORD

Fig. 64

View looking north to Mount Kinesava. The Moenkopi Formation is the lower red slope. The Shinarump Conglomerate, a member of the Chinle Formation, forms the tan cliff above the Moenkopi Formation upon which the Rockville Bench has been formed. The slopes beyond are formed on the Petrified Forest Member of the Chinle Formation, the Moenave Formation, and the Kayenta Formation. The thin red cliff in the middle of this slope is the Springdale Sandstone Member of the Moenave Formation. The top red and white cliff is the Navajo Sandstone.

Chinle Formation
(LATE TRIASSIC)

The streams that washed away some of the upper Moenkopi sediments deposited a blanket of cross-bedded sand and gravel over an area of roughly 260,000 km² (100,000 square miles) in the Southwest. This deposit, now cemented with quartz, is called the Shinarump Conglomerate. This distinctive light tan ledge former, up to 60 m (200 feet) thick over the area, is the lower member of the Chinle Formation (see Figure 64.)

The Chinle Formation is about 120 to 150 m (400 to 500 feet) thick in Zion National Park, and the upper member (the Petrified Forest Member) consists of approximately 90 m (300 feet) of variegated gray, purple and white shale with several light-colored sandstone and limestone layers. The shale has weathered to very loose clay forming a "badlands" topography of bare clay hills. The clay is mainly bentonite, a decomposition product of volcanic ash which swells considerably when wet and shrinks when drying. Upper Chinle terrain tends to slump and provides a notoriously unstable foundation for homes and other structures.

Chinle rocks (it seems incongruous to call the upper shales "rock" because they are so soft) are also noted for the petrified wood they contain. While not of "gem" quality here, as it is in the same formation at Petrified Forest National Park,

V. L. JACKSON

it is of great value in determining the environment of late Triassic time. The logs are invariably found in the horizontal position in the Shinarump, showing that they were carried as driftwood by the streams. Stewart, Poole and Wilson (1957) measured dip directions of Shinarump cross-beds and showed that these streams moved across this area from the east and southeast. Thus the pebbles and perhaps some of the logs in the Shinarump deposits were probably derived from highlands in Colorado and New Mexico.

Geologists have long been puzzled by the Shinarump because it is hard to imagine that fast-moving streams capable of carrying gravel and large trees perhaps more than 320 km (200 miles) could have formed on a gently sloping coastal plain. It is possible that uplift occurred inland, tipping the land surface and giving the streams added velocity. Might these deposits represent an enormous "Mount St. Helens" event far to the east?

The notion of nearby uplift and volcanism is supported by the evidence of volcanic ash (the bentonite in the upper Chinle), and, though the location of those volcanoes is unknown, it is believed that they were triggered by the crustal movements associated with the breakup of Pangaea. The abundance of soluble silica and other minerals from volcanic ash in the upper Chinle has been responsible for the petrification and the remarkable coloration of the fossil wood.

Gregory (1950) lists *Araucarioxylon* and *Woodworthia* as two common varieties of Chinle wood found here. The logs were probably derived from the highlands to the east, carried by the fast-moving streams, and deposited as driftwood on gravel bars.

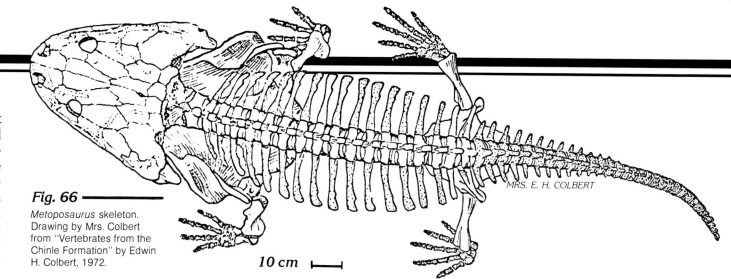

MRS. E. H. COLBERT

Fig. 66 ━━━━━

Metoposaurus skeleton. Drawing by Mrs. Colbert from "Vertebrates from the Chinle Formation" by Edwin H. Colbert, 1972.

10 cm ┣━━┫

A more level surface developed during late Chinle time, supporting a quiet water environment of marshes and ponds. Fossilized bone collected in upper Chinle shales near Cougar Mountain by Helmut Ehrenspeck has been identified by E. H. Colbert as the shoulder girdle of *Metoposaurus,* a large amphibian (see Figure 66).

The relative abundance of fresh water in the environment during Chinle time suggests that the slow northward drift of North America now placed Zion in the influence of a belt of heavy rainfall north of the equator. Zion now occupied a position like that of Sierra Leone and other west coast rain forested parts of Africa.

The Chinle Formation is also truncated at the top by a gentle erosional surface. This surface is marked by a change from soft purple and gray to the stronger red and brown coloration of the Moenave Formation above.

━**Fig. 67**

Fossil fragments of shoulder girdle of *Metoposaurus* from the Chinle Formation near Cougar Mountain. Found by Helmut Ehrenspeck, identified by E. H. Colbert.

V. L. JACKSON

Moenave Formation
(LATE TRIASSIC OR EARLY JURASSIC)

The Moenave Formation is from 120 to 170 m (400 to 570 feet) thick in the area of the Park, and it consists mainly of a lower member of reddish siltstone, which forms a slope, and an upper member of purplish-pink sandstone, which forms a prominent ledge over 30 m (100 feet) high. The lower member, called the Dinosaur Canyon Member, contains excellent ripple marks and cross-bedding characteristic of deposition by low energy streams and in ponded drainages. The upper sandstone, called the Springdale Member, represents stream deposition in an environment of greater stream discharges with faster moving water (see Figure 41).

Between the upper and lower members is the thin Whitmore Point Member, consisting of gray mudstone and shale, which was almost certainly deposited in an environment of ponds and lakes. Peterson has found palynomorphs (pollens and spores) in the Whitmore Point Member that have Jurassic affinities. In Oak Creek Canyon near the Visitor Center, there is a large lens-shaped deposit of clay clasts (actually clay gravel) in the Springdale Sandstone that shows that the sediments of a nearby Whitmore Point lake were ripped away in a flood and redeposited nearby during Springdale time.

The Moenave streams and ponds were inhabited by fish, as shown by fossilized remains of *Semionotus* (Figure 69) found at the base of the Springdale cliff near Pine Creek. *Semionotus's* modern relatives are the gar and sturgeon.

The continued abundance of water, though gypsum indicates occasional aridity, suggests that an equatorial climate still prevailed in Zion. At the end of Moenave time stream discharge diminished and the fine sands and silt of the Kayenta Formation were laid down.

Fig. 68

A mud-clast horizon is seen in the lower part of the cliff on the left, the Springdale Member of the Moenave. It is indicative of torrential flooding.

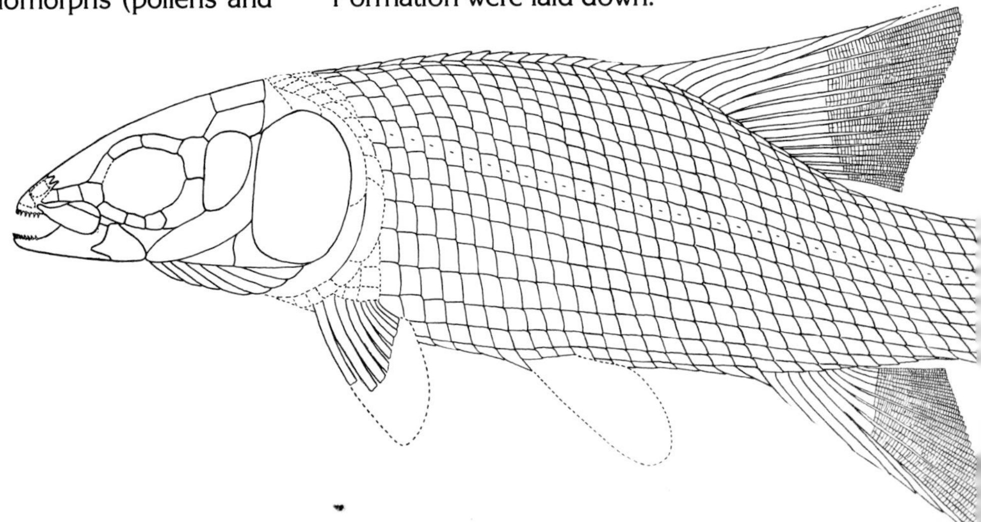

The contact between the Springdale Member and the Dinosaur Canyon Member of the Moenave Formation lies between the resistant sandstone at the top and the weaker siltstone below.

Fig. 69

Semionotus kanabensis, a gar-like fish similar to one described by Hesse (1935) from the Moenave strata in Zion Canyon. The somewhat rectangular scales are diagnostic. This individual was about 7 cm (3 inches) long, but the Zion skeleton was much larger.

Reproduced by permission of the Smithsonian Institution from "A Semionotoid Fish from the Chinle Formation, with Consideration of its Relationships", by B. Schaeffer and D. Dunkle, Smithsonian Institution, Washington, D.C.

Kayenta Formation
(EARLY JURASSIC)

Fig. 70 ———————

Saurian track (from a small dinosaur) from the Kayenta Formation in the Left Fork of North Creek.

The red and mauve Kayenta siltstones and sandstones that form the slopes at the base of the Navajo Sandstone cliffs record the deposition of low to moderate energy streams. Poole (1961) has shown that the streams still flowed from the east depositing from 150 to 210 m (500 to about 700 feet) of sediment here. The sedimentary structures showing the channel and flood plain deposits of streams are well exposed on the switchbacks below the tunnel in Pine Creek Canyon.

In the southeastern part of the Park a stratum of cross-bedded sandstone is found roughly halfway between the top and bottom of the Kayenta Formation. It is a "tongue" of dune sandstone that merges with the Navajo Formation east of Kanab, and it shows that desert conditions occurred briefly in this area during Kayenta time. This tongue is the ledge that shades the lower portion of the Emerald Pool Trail, and it is properly called Navajo, not Kayenta.

Fossil mud cracks attest to occasional seasonal climate, and thin limestones and fossilized trails of aquatic snails or worms mark the existence of ponds and lakes. The most interesting fossils, however, are the dinosaur tracks that are relatively common in Kayenta mudstone.

These vary in size, but all seem to be the tracks of three-toed reptiles that walked upright, leaving their tracks in the muds on the flood plains. Unfortunately, so far no bone materials have been found in the Park that would enable more specific identification.

Apparently during Kayenta time Zion was situated in a climatic belt like that of Senegal with rainy summers and dry winters at the southern edge of a great desert. The influence of the desert was about to predominate, however, as North America drifted northward into the arid west coast tropics.

Fig. 71

A large dinosaur track from the Kayenta Formation in the Left Fork of North Creek.

Navajo Formation
(EARLY JURASSIC)

Fig. 72
Cross-bedding in the Navajo Sandstone in the Narrows of the North Fork of the Virgin River. With minor exceptions this exposure shows dune structures formed by wind blowing from left to right in the photo.

The most outstanding sedimentary features in Zion are the cross-bed sets of the Navajo Sandstone, particularly in the upper part of the formation. These diagonal sweeping lines mark the advance (perhaps daily) of great dunes across a lowland desert. The sandstone is almost completely devoid of fossils over its entire area of outcrop, desert not being noted for abundant life, nor for conditions suitable for fossilization. The Navajo desert environment spread sand over an area of about 390,000 km² (150,000 square miles), stretching from central Wyoming to southeastern California, but the maximum thickness of the sands, about 670 m (2,200 feet), was reached in Zion.

Marzolf (1970) argues convincingly that the flat-bedded sandstone and siltstone in the lowest part of the Navajo in Zion have to some extent accumulated under the influence of water at the sea coast and by streams. I think that this is compatible with the idea that the desert influence was moving southeastward into this area as the continent continued its northward drift. Summer rains would have gradually moved farther into the area of dune accumulation, transporting sand and redepositing it along the southern edge of the desert. Marzolf sees the influence of water expressed in the structures of the middle part of the Navajo as well. Slumped cross-bedding seems to indicate that dunes were at times inundated, perhaps by the nearby sea. The impression of a desert by the sea is strengthened by the occurrence of thin dolomite strata in the middle part of the formation. These layers suggest ponding and evaporation of sea water.

The cross-bedded upper part of the Navajo, that seen along the Zion-Mt. Carmel Highway east of the small tunnel, appears to be almost entirely wind deposited sand. Marzolf shows from the direction of dip of the cross-bed sets that the wind direction was generally northerly (between northeasterly and north-northwesterly) in the upper Navajo of southern Utah. This is compatible with the prevailing wind directions to be expected in the zone of northeast trade winds of west coast tropical deserts in the northern hemisphere. During Navajo time Zion probably occupied a position like that of the Spanish Sahara.

The quartz sand grains of the Navajo Desert became very well rounded by the action of the driving winds. This is apparent when the loose grains of sand are examined with a handlens. Rounded grains are indicated also in a way that is not altogether pleasant. Where the trails of the Park traverse the Navajo Sandstone, a thin deposit of sand grains often accumulates just where you need secure footing. Unless you are prepared, you may be surprised to find that your foot slips on this layer of miniature ball bearings. This is why the trail surface is paved in many places.

Viewed with a microscope, the well-rounded quartz sand grains appear frosted, that is their surfaces seem to have suffered repeated sharp impacts *without the cushioning effect of water.* This has been one of the arguments for a desert origin of the Navajo dune structures. Marzolf

(1970) has cast doubt on this interpretation by examining the grains with the higher magnification of a scanning electron microscope. His photographs show that the "frosted" surface is actually etched. Apparently post-depositional influences have altered the grain surfaces, somewhat obscuring the depositional history.

Fig. 73

Dune in a modern desert in Death Valley National Monument. Wind direction is from right to left.

Temple Cap Formation
(EARLY MID-JURASSIC)

Streams carrying red mud flooded the Navajo Desert for a brief time, beveling the dune terrain to a gently undulating surface and depositing a few meters of clay and silt. Then desert conditions gradually resumed for a short time. These events are recorded by the caprock at the tops of the East Temple and West Temple and elsewhere in the area.

This influx of water caused the underlying Navajo sand (not yet cemented with calcite) to slump. Silica-cemented fracture and slump structures are ubiquitous in the uppermost Navajo throughout the Park.

84

The Temple Cap Formation is a thin, white sandstone layer deposited during a brief resumption of desert environment after Navajo time. Above, the formation rests on the bench in the massive white Navajo cliffs.

Slump structures in the Temple Cap (left) are visible from the East Rim Trail. The Temple Cap is also exposed on top of the West Temple (right), the type locality for this formation.

Carmel Formation
(MID-JURASSIC)

Again red muds were deposited (now on the Temple Cap sands) by streams that planed the surface, creating another unconformity. Again the water produced slump features in the underlying sand. But now the area was once again submerged as the crust sagged and the sea moved in from the west. The Carmel Formation records a varied history of sedimentary accumulation with light tan and light gray limestones (Limestone Member) over the lower red clay, then banded pink and tan earthy sandstone (Banded Member), then (in places) thick gypsum (Gypsiferous Member), then the gray and pink-banded earthy sandstone (the Windsor Member), possibly aeolian in origin. The Carmel Formation is about 260 m (850 feet) thick in this area.

The limestone contains fossils of unquestionable marine origin. Crinoids, pectens, clams and oysters are relatively common. Oolitic limestone containing bivalves and snails is seen along the Wildcat Canyon Trail.* A few nondiagnostic marine fossils are present above the gypsum (Gregory, 1950). The environment apparently alternated between shallow marine and coastal desert with an extended interval of evaporite deposition of gypsum. Anhydrite crystal impressions are found in some of the limestone.

The upper member of the Carmel Formation contains small, angular fragments of volcanic rock which appear not to have been transported a great distance (their edges are not rounded off). It is tempting to think that they may record the beginning of igneous activity to the west. As will be seen in the next chapter, there is evidence of local crustal movement at about this time.

Late Jurassic rocks are not represented here. They have been removed by erosion which produced an angular unconformity at the top of the Carmel Formation. The Mesozoic Era ended in Zion in a more definite fashion than it began, with uplift, erosion and perhaps associated volcanic activity.

---

*Oolites are tiny algal balls formed in very shallow tropical seawater, for example in the Bahamas and Florida Bay in Everglades National Park.

J. L. CRAWFORD

V. L. JACKSON

1 cm

Dakota Formation
(UPPER? CRETACEOUS)

JAMES E. STAEBLER

A small area of Dakota rocks outcrops in the northwest corner of the Park at the top of Horse Ranch Mountain. The Dakota is much better represented north and east of the Park, but on Horse Ranch Mountain a basal conglomerate and tan fossiliferous sandstone (with impressions of terrestrial plants and pelecypods) are characteristic of the Dakota. Brown (1973) and Moir (1974) state that the source area for the Dakota sediments was to the west. This points to a reversal in the regional slope and uplift in the west in what throughout the Mesozoic had been an area occupied by shallow seas. Thus the unconformity above the Carmel probably represents a long interval of erosion. More on this in the next chapter.

In very brief fashion we have followed the changes in environment recorded in the rocks of Zion over an interval of more than one hundred million years. In that interval, Zion occupied a west coastal position until the end. The sedimentary record spans a period of emergence from below a shallow sea, resubmergence and re-emergence. The sediments and their structures seem to faithfully record a history of slow drift of the continent over a distance of roughly 3,200 km (2,000 miles) and about 27 degrees of latitude. The most outstanding evidence of the slow drift through climatic belts is the unrivaled Navajo Sandstone with its dune structures so clearly seen today in Zion.

Fig. 74 (above)
Horse Ranch Mountain and Paria Point from Beatty Point. The red cliffs of Navajo Sandstone are overlain by light gray limestones and gypsum of the Carmel Formation. The Cretaceous Dakota Formation outcrops near the mountain top and is covered by Quaternary(?)-age basalt at the summit.

Fig. 75 (far left)
Fossil clams *(Unio)* from the Carmel Formation north of Kolob Reservoir.

Fig. 76 (left)
Isocrinus fossils from the Carmel Formation near Mt. Carmel Junction. These are fragments of marine animals called crinoids.

The Dakota Formation lies at the very top of Horse Ranch Mountain (right) under a thin basalt cap in the vegetated area.

V. L. JACKSON

Red sunsets much like this one over Springdale, Utah, just outside the South Entrance of the Park, were caused by ash discharged from ancient volcanoes.

HISTORY OF DEFORMATION 4

The art of representation, then, is a long way from reality.

PLATO

Relation of Art to Truth

The strata of Zion at the western edge of the Colorado Plateau are so undeformed relative to the Basin and Range Province to the west, or the Rocky Mountains to the east, that much of our area is said to have a "layer cake" geology. We have seen, however, how important the gentle dip, faulting and jointing of strata have been in determining the erosional outcome. Zion would not have become the place that it is if not for the moderate deformation which has affected the region during the past hundred million years.

Moreover the manifestations of our "restless Earth" are worthy of interest, whether here at the block faulted boundary between the Basin and Range and Colorado Plateau Provinces or in highly deformed mountainous regions. Let us delve into the history of crustal movement in Zion and the nearby area and see if developments affecting our "layer cake" are as amenable to understanding as the simple structures might at first imply. I hope that no one will be disappointed to learn that we do not as yet have "the" answer.

The truth is that while some of the developments can be pieced together from field evidence, much remains to be understood.

The general picture of tectonism in the Southwest during the time of interest here is one of crustal compression and uplift, beginning perhaps in middle Mesozoic time and culminating with major erosion during Cretaceous time, followed by stretching of the crust since the mid-Cenozoic. The latter extensional activity affected a broad belt extending through Nevada and into the adjoining states north and south.

The manifestations of these events have already been briefly described and include such features as joints, high angle faults, low angle thrust faults and folds. Also large areas of the crust have been tipped, either by vertical displacement on fault planes which has allowed tilting of crustal slabs, or by regional upwarp or downwarp involving only bending. In the following sections the processes which led to development of these features are described.

Compression

Perhaps as early as Temple Cap time, during the Jurassic period roughly 150 million years ago, western North America began to "feel" a push from the west. This roughly east-west compression between the North American crust and the Pacific crust progressed until a break occurred along the western edge of the continental shelf and the Pacific Ocean floor began to slide underneath North America.

This concept of plates overlapping in compression has been widely accepted among geologists who subscribe to the theory of plate tectonics. Apparently, as the western oceanic plate glided beneath the continent, low density sedimentary material was dragged along and added to the bottom of the continental crust in western North America. If you were to see this happening with slabs of ice on a windswept pond, you would notice that it would cause the edge of the "continent" slab to rise due to the added buoyancy of the underthrust slab. This occurred on a large scale in the west in a more complex manner than implied here, and our part of the Southwest began to be squeezed, gently folded and broadly uplifted as early as perhaps 150 million years ago. The immediate area has been elevated by more than 3,200 m (10,500 feet) over the past 60 million years.

Rock can yield like putty or modeling clay to the forces of compression if the stresses are applied gradually enough, which is apparently what happened in the northwest corner of the Park. The Kanarra Fold in the Kolob Canyons area is a north-northeastward trending anticline, formed in the same manner as a wrinkle in a rug which covers a slippery floor.

Kurie (1966) thought that the Kanarra Fold may have been formed in late Carmel time. This writer believes that the thinning (slower deposition) of the Temple Cap Formation in the vicinity of the fold zone may imply even earlier arching along the anticline. The Kanarra Fold is aligned with the Virgin anticline, Harrisburg Dome and other domes at Washington and Bloomington (near St. George), and it is believed they all formed at about the same time.

If compressive stresses are applied rapidly enough, deformation takes place by development of thrust faults. Fractures occur which allow a slab of the crust to be thrust over itself. The Kanarra Fold is broken on its eastern flank by the Taylor Creek Thrust Zone here, and one sees two Springdale Sandstone ledges in vertical succession when looking north along the thrust zone from the Taylor Creek Road. The upper plate* of the thrust block has moved from the east toward the west.

---

*Here the term "plate" is used in a more local sense than previously. A thrust plate is only a few kilometers thick and covers an area of only a few tens or hundreds of square kilometers.

Fig. 77

Cross-sectional view of a compressional plate boundary. Oceanic crust consisting of basic volcanic rocks overlain by marine sediment is being thrust underneath continental crust. This is called a subduction zone. Notice how the massive sediments are folded and broken as they are carried down to great depths beneath the continental block. There, under intense heat and pressure, they are converted to metamorphic rock or in some cases melted. When subduction stops, these low density rocks are elevated by buoyancy, lifting and buckling the thick continental crust. They may later be exposed by erosion, forming the igneous and metamorphic roofs of mountain ranges such as the Rocky Mountains and the Sierra Nevada.

A

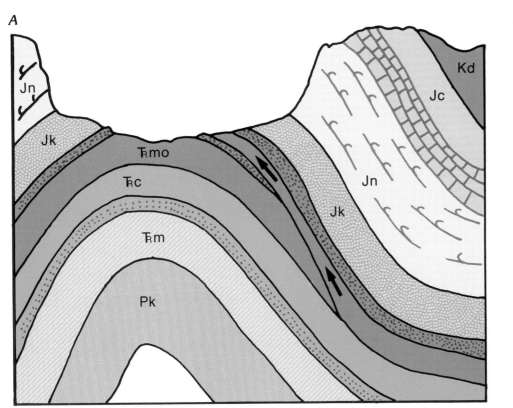

B

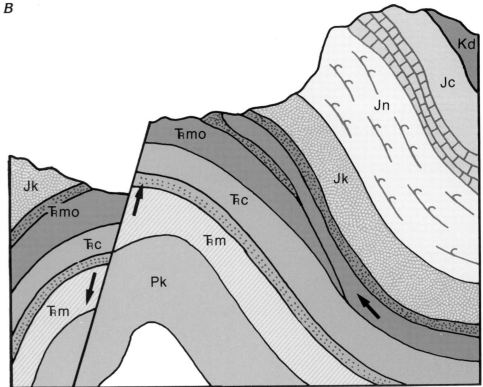

In my opinion the thrusting occurred long after the extended period of compression which produced the folds, perhaps in mid-Tertiary time or later as a consequence of gravity sliding. You will recall that dipping strata, especially those overlying incompetent clays, are subject to down-slope sliding under the influence of gravity. In other areas even large-scale folded belts and thrust zones have been explained in this way.

Perhaps this interpretation can be used to explain the fact that evidence of west-to-east thrusting (opposite to that described above) is found along the western limb of the fold belt in the vicinity of Silver Reef and Harrisburg Junction west of the Park.

Northwest of Currant Creek the east-to-west Taylor Creek Thrust Zone is overlain by west-to-east displaced strata on the eastern flank of the

fold. Kurie (1966) drew attention to this, but I would like to emphasize the fact that the reversal in direction of thrusting is accompanied by well-developed west-to-east drag folding in the Spring-dale Sandstone, indicating that a considerable thickness of strata was involved. To me this says that this west-to-east gravity sliding occurred after the Taylor Creek Thrust, yet well over a million years ago, and certainly earlier than the volcan-

Fig. 78

Cross sections looking north through the Kanarra Fold in the northwestern part of Zion. *A)* Arrows show how the Moenave Formation was broken and thrust over itself from east to west, "doubling" itself on the east flank of the fold. *B)* The arrows show displacement along the Hurricane Fault, with rocks on the west displaced downward.

Folds formed by compressive thrusting of rock from the east stand exposed in Taylor Creek.

DODGE

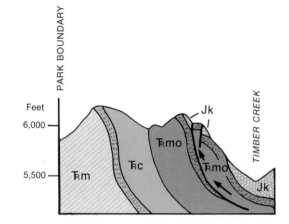

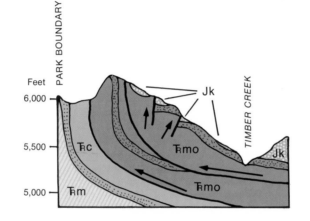

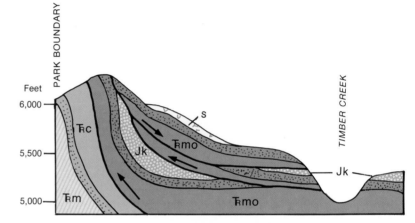

Fig. 79

Cross-section views looking northward through the east flank of the Kanarra Fold in the northwestern part of Zion National Park. The successive views, starting in the vicinity of the Kolob Canyons Scenic Drive and extending south to the area of Pace Knoll, show the complexity of the overthrust block of the Taylor Creek Thrust. Two thrust plates are evident in many places along the thrust zone.

ism responsible for the Black Ridge basalt which unconformably overlies the thrust zone west of Currant Creek.

The Kolob Canyons east of the Taylor Creek Thrust Zone appear to have been eroded along tear faults formed in the upper east-to-west thrust plate. One remnant of a tear fault may be seen in the Carmel Formation at the head of the canyon of the Middle Fork of Taylor Creek. Another possible tear fault swings into the head of Camp Creek from the north and west. Although direct evidence is lacking, it appears that La Verkin Creek, between Burnt Mountain and Gregory Butte, lies along another tear fault in which the north block is raised in relation to strata to the south.

Igneous activity often accompanies phases of such compressive deformation and sometimes

helps to date such events. The igneous rocks usually produced during compression are relatively rich in silica, indicating that crustal rocks are being melted and injected through fractured zones forming strato-volcanoes which blanket the surface with the ejecta of explosive eruptions. Armstrong and Higgins (1973) have summarized the results of radiometric dating of western volcanic rocks and have shown that such igneous activity moved into the area just west of Zion between 20 and 30 million years ago. Their analysis suggests a pattern of compressive stresses creeping into the area from the northwest. As it takes time for such viscous magma to work its way through to the surface, the associated maximum of compressive deformation is thought to have occurred somewhat earlier than 30 million years ago. Rowley *et al.* (1978) would place these events at least 50 million years before present.

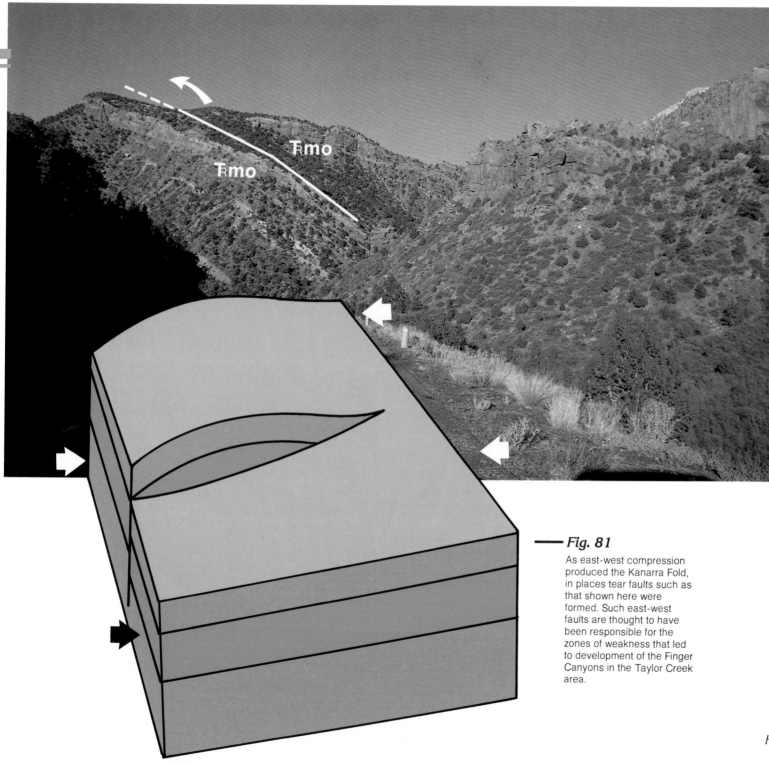

Tmo

Tmo

— *Fig. 80*

View northward along the Taylor Creek Thrust Zone showing how the Moenave Formation has been thrust westward upon itself. The Springdale Sandstone forms a prominent ledge in the overriding block and again in the overriden block.

— *Fig. 81*

As east-west compression produced the Kanarra Fold, in places tear faults such as that shown here were formed. Such east-west faults are thought to have been responsible for the zones of weakness that led to development of the Finger Canyons in the Taylor Creek area.

Extension

Sometime after about 20 million years ago the crustal stresses near Zion, particularly in Nevada to the west, became extensional. The crust was now being gently pulled apart in a roughly east-west direction. In Nevada this produced an array of north-south trending mountain blocks separated by graben valleys. This tensional deformation was manifested to a lesser extent in the development of north-northwest trending normal faults and associated basaltic volcanism in Zion and vicinity. Figure 82 is a cross section showing the association of Crater Hill, a volcanic cinder cone, and the south end of the Cougar Mountain graben west of the West Temple.

Such deformation occurs on crustal plate boundaries which are active zones of rifting or spreading. Usually such zones are found in ocean basins where new crust is being formed by magma derived from the mantle. Volcanoes in these zones produce basaltic lava which is low in silica content. The East Pacific Rise is a submarine mountain range formed along a spreading zone. Apparently over the past 20 million years the North American crust has moved westward over this rift, and the continental crust has been pulled apart in much the same fashion as linoleum laid over a sagging floor. The Cougar Mountain faults and those that trend north-northwestward through Wildcat Canyon and across Echo Canyon, as well as the Beartrap Fault, are all high-angle normal faults of relatively recent origin.

There are several instances in which volcanic cinder cones and associated vents are located on or very near these normal faults. No doubt the lava found its way to the surface along the fractured fault zones in these cases. Home Valley Knoll (a cinder cone just outside the Park boundary west of Lava Point) lies on the Wildcat Canyon Fault. Firepit Knoll, Spendlove Knoll and several older vents and small cones lie on or very near to the East Cougar Mountain Fault. Crater Hill lies near the southern end of the West Cougar Mountain Fault.

In the case of the East Cougar Mountain Fault a long time lag is indicated between faulting and volcanism. Upland canyons have developed along the fault trace, suggesting that erosion occurred in the fault zone for somewhat less than a million years following displacement. Upper

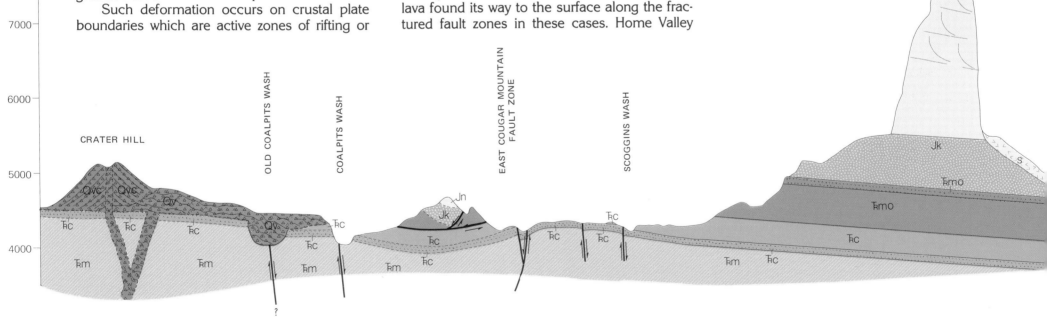

96

Fig. 82

Cross section looking northward through the southern part of the Cougar Mountain graben, near Crater Hill just west of the West Temple. The West Cougar Mountain Fault passes through Coalpits Wash at this point. "Qv" and "Qvc" are Quaternary basalt and basaltic cinders. The other formation name symbols are the same as given in Figure 3. Vertical exaggeration X2.

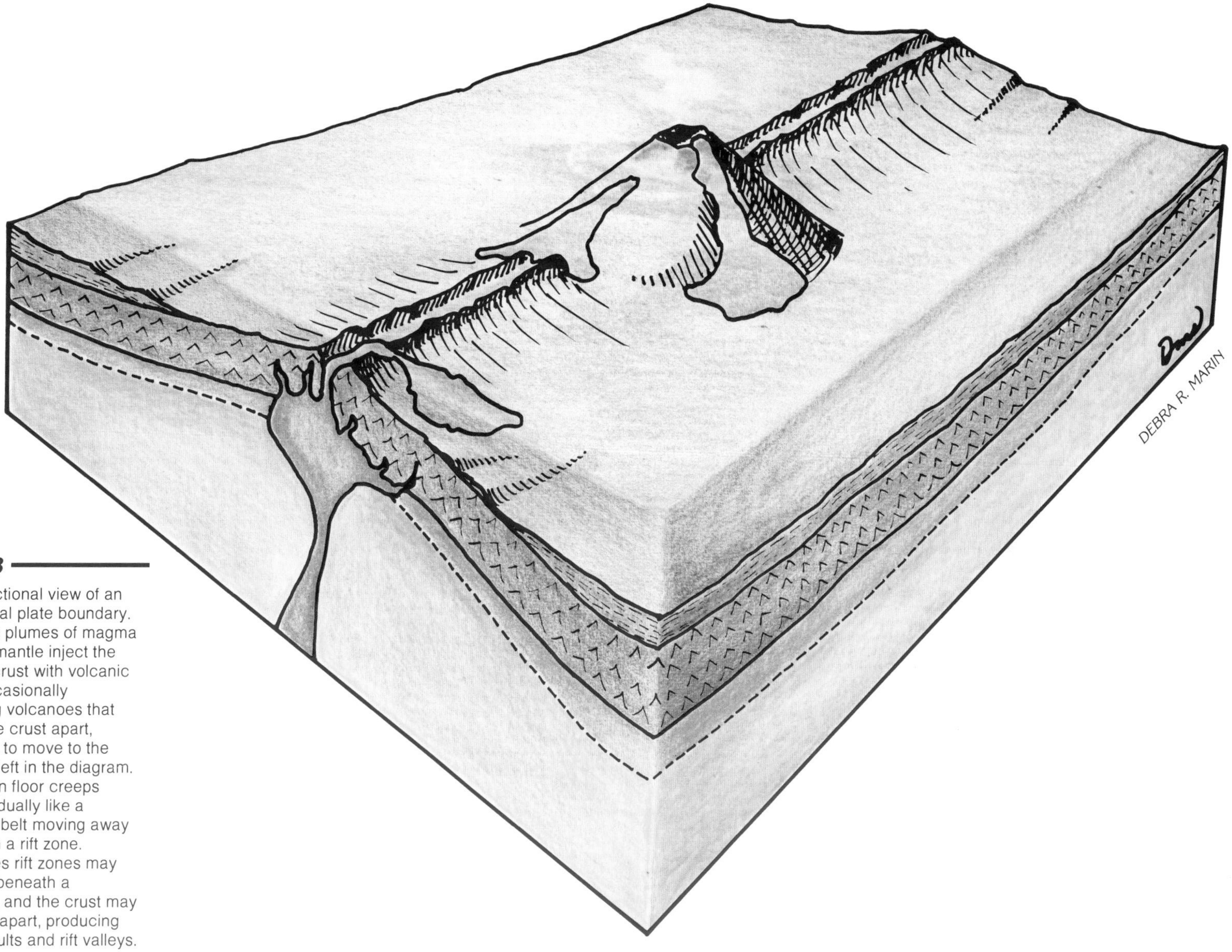

Fig. 83

Cross sectional view of an extensional plate boundary. Upwelling plumes of magma from the mantle inject the oceanic crust with volcanic dikes, occasionally producing volcanoes that wedge the crust apart, causing it to move to the right and left in the diagram. The ocean floor creeps along gradually like a conveyor belt moving away from such a rift zone. Sometimes rift zones may originate beneath a continent, and the crust may be pulled apart, producing normal faults and rift valleys.

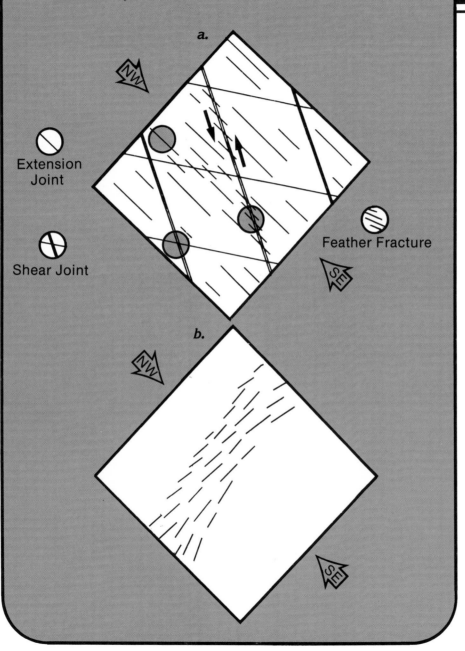

Fig. 84

A) Joints formed by northwest-southeast compression. The NNW-SSE set of shear joints and associated feather fractures seem to dominate in the Navajo Sandstone. Small arrows show direction of shear responsible for feather fractures. **B)** Swarm of joints formed over the crest of an anticline produced by NW-SE compression.

Hop Valley and Lee Valley have subsequently been flooded by basalts. The 0.26 million year (m.y.) age of the basalt at Grapevine Spring can be used to estimate the age of the East Cougar Mountain Fault at approximately one million years before present. The displacement on this fault is approximately 150 m (500 feet) at Cougar Mountain.

The Wildcat Canyon Fault is covered by the Lava Point flows (0.7 m.y. according to Best), but the flows are not displaced by the fault. As no appreciable pre-flow canyon is evident in this fault zone, fault movement may have predated volcanic activity by only a relatively short time.

The pronounced jog in the North Creek flows at the confluence of the Left and Right Forks of North Creek suggests that erosion had occurred along the zone of the West Cougar Mountain Fault for at least a few hundred thousand years prior to nearby volcanic activity. Again it seems that faulting significantly predated volcanism.

Perhaps the only exception to this apparent relationship is the Beartrap Fault. With over 275 meters (900 feet) of displacement, it is believed significant that the scarp canyon contains no remnants of the flows from the large volcano two miles to the east. That volcano is believed to have been responsible for the Malony Hill flow, dating at 1.4 m.y., so the Beartrap Fault may be younger than this.

Evidence of most recent faulting in the area comes from outside the Park. Hamblin et al. (1975) reported an offset of 130 m (440 feet) on 0.25 m.y. old basalt along the Hurricane Fault at La Verkin. This episode was roughly synchronous with the North Creek volcanism. A small displacement of recent alluvium (presumably

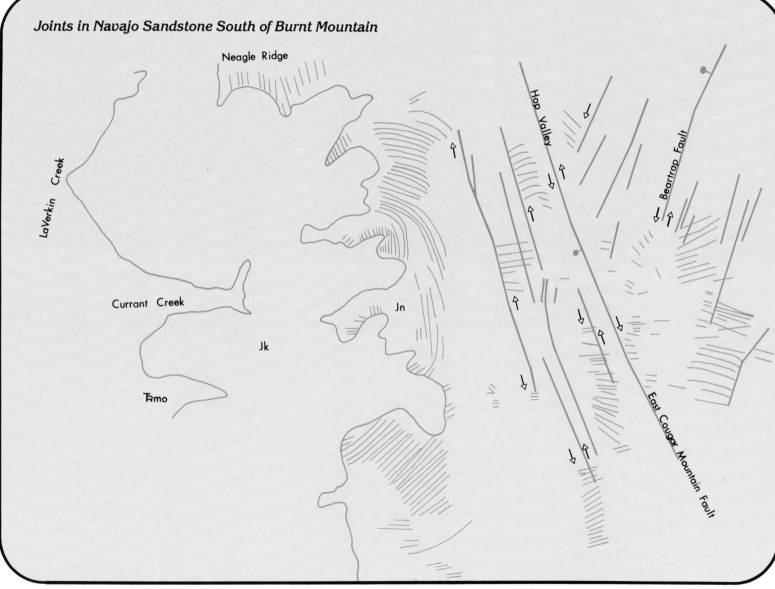

Joints in Navajo Sandstone South of Burnt Mountain

Neagle Ridge

LaVerkin Creek

Currant Creek

Jk

Jn

Ŧmo

Hop Valley

Beartrap Fault

East Cougar Mountain Fault

GREER CHESHER

— *Fig. 85*

Joints in Navajo Sandstone south of Burnt Mountain. Thrust plate pile-up against Kanarra Fold produced a concentric joint pattern except where relieved by development of East Cougar Mountain Fault and associated parallel shear zones. Beartrap Fault and its parallel shear zones served a similar stress-release function. Direction of shear is indicated by arrows. Fault lines are shown by heavy lines. Bar and ball are on down-thrown side of faults. Compare with Figure 35.

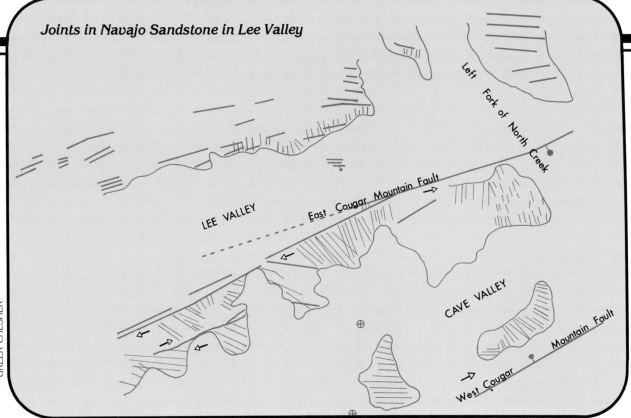

Joints in Navajo Sandstone in Lee Valley

LEFT FORK OF NORTH CREEK

EAST COUGAR MOUNTAIN FAULT

LEE VALLEY

CAVE VALLEY

WEST COUGAR MOUNTAIN FAULT

Fig. 86

Joints in Navajo Sandstone near East Cougar Mountain Fault at Lee Valley. Contact lines demark the limit of exposure of Navajo Sandstone. Arrows indicate direction of shear suggested by joint pattern, dotted where inferred. Cinder cones are indicated by ⊕. Fault lines are shown by heavy lines. Bar and ball are on downthrown side of faults. See Figure 35 for comparison.

younger than about 10,000 years) by slippage in the Hurricane Fault zone near Pintura has been reported by Kurie (1966).

The largest normal faults near the Park, the displacements on which have most profoundly influenced erosional activity here, are the Sevier and Hurricane faults, forming respectively the east and west margins of the Markagunt Plateau block. Hundreds of meters of displacement on these faults has tipped the plateau toward the northeast, imparting to the sedimentary strata a gentle dip in that direction. It is believed that the tipping has occurred in stages throughout the past 20 million years.

The irregular line of white Navajo cliffs one

encounters when traveling eastward toward Zion from the fault line near Hurricane is a retreating erosional escarpment. The position of this escarpment east of the fault is a measure of the length of time elapsed since the greatest amount of fault movement. The fact that the Navajo cliffs trend away from the fault farther south in the Park tells us that the fault slipped earlier near La Verkin than in the Taylor Creek area.

Active faulting tends to migrate along such zones. In recent decades earthquakes, signifying small displacements, have occurred farther north along this zone on the Wasatch Front. During historical time southwestern Utah has been relatively inactive seismically. Yet evidence shows that this was a land of earthquakes in the past, and there is no reason to think that these faults may not become reactivated in the future. When seismic activity resumes Zion will be a particularly dangerous place.

Let us now consider the jointing so remarkably well displayed in the Navajo Sandstone in this historical context. Unfortunately, geologists do not as yet thoroughly understand the mechanism of joint formation. It is difficult to deduce from the geometry of jointing the orientation of the stresses that caused the fracturing. At least to this geologist the origin of the jointing in the Navajo is still beclouded with uncertainty.

Perhaps in the final analysis an investigation of the rock cleavage in the shaly sediments underlying the Navajo will prove more accurate in determining the directions of the stresses involved. Until such a study is done we are restricted to a consideration of two alternative hypotheses, namely: 1) the joints are a result of the relaxation of compressive stresses acquired by the rock during late Mesozoic squeezing, or 2) they were formed by tensile stresses during the late Cenozoic interval of extension.

Figures 84 through 87 show how several patterns of joints might be formed following compression. Of the several sets that might be expected in theory, four sets are well developed in the Navajo. The majority of long, well formed joints in the Park are rather widely spaced, being several hundred meters apart on average, and they are the joints responsible for the parallel array of tributary canyons intersecting the Parunuweap, Clear Creek, Echo Canyon and Orderville Canyon drainages (see Figure 20).

Between many pairs of the north-northwest set are other joints that I call feather fractures. These are shorter and much more closely spaced, being generally less than a hundred meters apart in aerial view. Often they intersect the north-northwest set at angles close to ninety degrees. In other cases, they appear to curve toward a north-northwest strike direction and assume an attitude similar to that of the widely spaced set. The feather fractures are like those formed on vertical slabs which are shearing against each other horizontally along the north-northwest joint planes. If so, the impression from Eardley's joint map (Figure 35) is that the western part of the Park was gliding south-south-eastward with respect to the eastern part.

Thirdly, there are sets of meandering joints west of Burnt Mountain and an array of east-northeast striking joints in Parunuweap Canyon that appear to be extension joints formed over the crests of anticlines or monoclines (a monocline is a stairstep-shaped fold).

Finally there is a non-vertical joint set commonly seen on cliff faces. This type is well exhibited on the face of Cable Mountain where the joint planes strike roughly northeast, dip approximately 60 to 70 degrees and form huge X patterns on the wall seen from Weeping Rock. These joints seem to have been formed by relaxation or extension in an east-west direction.

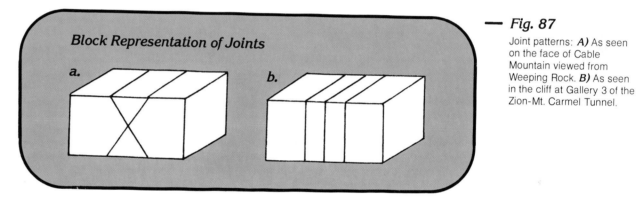

Block Representation of Joints

a.

b.

One important attribute of the principal north-northwest joint set is that they are aligned with the faults which developed during Pliocene and Pleistocene time when the region was subjected to extensional stresses. Perhaps most of these joints, and the associated feather fractures, were formed at about the same time as the normal faults.

— *Fig. 87*

Joint patterns: *A)* As seen on the face of Cable Mountain viewed from Weeping Rock. *B)* As seen in the cliff at Gallery 3 of the Zion-Mt. Carmel Tunnel.

We have traced the history of Zion through nearly a quarter of a billion years, looking at analogues in today's world that would help us to understand how great thicknesses of sedimentary rocks were formed and shaped into what we now see. I hope that this trip has been as enjoyable for you as it has been for me, and I urge you to spend enough time in Zion to see some of the subtle and profound geological features that may not have been obvious to you when you first arrived. Better yet, try to look more deeply into the rocks to see the processes that have formed and shaped them. And, what I would hope more than this is that some of you, keeping in mind Plato's admonition at the beginning of this chapter, would investigate deeply enough to improve our overall understanding of the events that have occurred here.

ROAD GUIDE 5
TO GEOLOGY

Four geologic road guides are included
which assist in locating many of the strata and
other features on the ground as described in the
previous chapters. A copy of the "Geological Map
of Zion National Park, Utah" is an important aid
while in the field.

Collecting rock and fossil specimens is au-
thorized only through a collecting permit available at the visitor centers upon prior request. The
permit is issued only to persons from recognized
educational institutions performing necessary
and substantial research in the Park. Private col-
lections are not allowed.

Zion-Mt. Carmel Highway

ROY GIVEN

Checkerboard Mesa.

East Boundary:

DISTANCES EAST TO WEST	DISTANCES WEST TO EAST
0.0 km *(0.0 mi)*	20.6 km *(12.8 mi)*

The highway passes into the Park through the upland valley of Co-op Creek, which is developed in the Carmel, Temple Cap and upper Navajo Formations of early and middle Jurassic age. The contact between the Navajo and Temple Cap Formations is formed by the first bench, about 90 m (300 feet) above road level. At the base of the second bench, about 170 m (550 feet) above the highway, is the contact between the Temple Cap and Carmel Formations. The mesa tops and plateau are formed on the lower limestone member of the Carmel Formation. The lowest few meters of the Temple Cap and Carmel consist of deep reddish shale and silt.

Here as in most areas of outcrop the cross-bedded sandstones of the Navajo and Temple Cap are laced with silica cemented fractures, penetrating several meters into the upper beds of these formations and suggesting shrinkage and slump shortly after deposition.

Checkerboard Mesa Viewpoint

1.6 km *(1.0 mi)*	19.0 km *(11.8 mi)*

Two sets of grooves create the checkerboard pattern on the white sandstone face. The roughly horizontal set is formed along coarse sand units that truncate cross sets of windblown sand. The near vertical set, perpendicular to the first, is formed on shallow fractures caused by expansion and contraction of the surface rock. The stress may be due to freezing/thawing, heating/cooling, wetting/drying or perhaps all three processes. A polygonal set of fractures can be seen in places where the bedding is parallel to the exposed surface.

The best examples of dune cross-stratification in the Navajo are seen between here and the long tunnel. Side canyons are developed parallel to a system of north-northwest trending joints. Several pulloffs are provided with interpretive signs explaining these features.

Tunnel, east portal and head of Canyon Overlook Trail:

10.3 km *(6.4 mi)*	10.3 km *(6.4 mi)*

In many places between here and Checkerboard Mesa impressive accumulations of iron minerals may be seen along the roadway. These occur as brownish-black grapefruit sized concretions, reniform masses that form resistant caps on sandstone hoodoos, joint fillings and chocolate-brown "earthy" zones occurring as lenses in the sandstone. It seems likely that this iron has been

Great Arch of Zion in Pine Creek Canyon.

removed by solution from the upper (now white) part of the Navajo and redeposited at this lower elevation by groundwater action, perhaps associated with hydrocarbons.

The tunnel passes through the lower 80 m (260 feet) of the Navajo Sandstone and within a few meters of the face of the south wall of Pine Creek Canyon. Completed in 1930 the tunnel represents a brave expression of rock engineering with galleries and windows providing views of Pine Creek Canyon. A large slab of rock broke away on the cliff face above Gallery 3 (the double window) in April of 1958, blocking the tunnel with debris. New reinforcement there was supporting a load of over 1.8 million kg per square meter (1.3 tons per square inch) in August 1978.

The Navajo-Kayenta contact is blanketed by talus at the west portal. The contact is considered to be essentially the base of the sandstone cliff. Some consider it to be the horizon where bed-

ding changes from flat- to cross-bedded upward in the lower few meters of the sandstone, but that leads to a problematical, irregular contact surface.

Turnout on right of second hairpin turn below tunnel:

13.5 km	*(8.4 mi)*	7.1 km	*(4.4 mi)*

Kayenta stream deposits are well exposed here on the road cut to the south, looking toward the west portal of the tunnel. An early Jurassic stream channel is indicated by the lens-shaped stratum of sandstone sandwiched between flood-plain silts.

A small normal fault is also exposed in the cut, displacing downward the east end of the channel deposit. The fault which can be traced to the largest tunnel window is believed to be inactive.

The switchbacks also traverse several large masses of rockslide debris, some of which still rolls onto the roadway from time to time.

Pine Creek Bridge:

17.2 km	*(10.7 mi)*	3.4 km	*(2.1 mi)*

Here you are level with the gray shales of the middle, Whitmore Point member of the late Triassic (or possibly Jurassic) Moenave Formation. The sandstone ledge just above road level is the Springdale Member. The reddish siltstones and sandstones of the Dinosaur Canyon Member outcrop beneath the gray shales. Scales of *Semionotus,* a freshwater fish, have been discovered nearby.

Approximately halfway up the irregular slopes below the Navajo is another prominent ledge. This is a tongue of Navajo Sandstone within the Kayenta beds. It represents a brief interval of dune intrusion that choked the streams with sand.

At the south end of the bridge there is a shallow cave in the Springdale ledge which contains unconsolidated silt and white marl strata. These are the only remaining deposits of Pine Creek Lake, formed about 4,000 years ago when a great slide from The Sentinel blocked the mouth of the canyon. The remains of the slide dam can be seen overlapping the Springdale ledge about 0.4 km (a quarter mile) to the west.

Between this point and the 13.5 km (8.4 mile) stop you can see a fresh scar on the Navajo cliff face above Gallery 3 of the tunnel where rock broke loose in April, 1958.

Canyon Junction:

18.0 km	(11.2 mi)	2.6 km	(1.6 mi)

The Scenic Drive up Zion Canyon begins here. Looking upstream, you see a huge slump and slide mass on the west side of the river, the North Fork of the Virgin. The debris is part of the slide from The Sentinel that blocked the river (and Pine Creek) about 4,000 years ago, producing a large lake in the canyon upstream.

Visitor Center:

19.1 km	(11.9 mi)	1.5 km	(0.9 mi)

The Visitor Center has books, weather forecasts, information and exhibits illustrating local geology and related subjects. Also, it is a good idea for safety to check in here if you plan to enter the backcountry.

From the front of the Visitor Center a free-standing arch of Navajo Sandstone may be seen on Bridge Mountain across the canyon. A tongue of Navajo Sandstone outcrops below the arch, about in the middle of the Kayenta section.

The view from the back of the Visitor Center is dominated by the West Temple and the Towers of the Virgin, the former appropriately capped by about 85 m (275 feet) of Temple Cap Formation overlain by a few feet of Carmel limestone. The greatest thickness of the Navajo Sandstone is attained here, an estimated 610 m (2,000 feet) at the head of Oak Creek Canyon.

The bench to the southwest, looking toward the West Temple, is capped with cemented slide material which probably predates Oak Creek Canyon. The orientation of large blocks of Navajo Sandstone in the debris suggests that the source of the slide was near Meridian Tower, north of Oak Creek.

Downcanyon from the Visitor Center in the campground area and Springdale and beyond, the canyon floor has a flat aspect that is due to infilling with stream alluvium. The cause of this alluviation may be linked to damming by a large slump block that moved down in segments from Johnson Mountain, a butte south of the Watch-

Moon over West Temple.

106

man. It is also possible that the damming effect of Crater Hill lava, near Grafton, was felt this far upcanyon.

South Entrance:

20.6 km	*(12.8 mi)*	0.0 km	*(0.0 mi)*

Here the west skyline is dominated by a bench of Moenave sandstone and siltstone. The ledge near the top of the bench is the Springdale Member of the Moenave Formation. It is overlain by about 60 m (200 feet) of Kayenta siltstone and sandstone, capped by a layer of cemented slide debris. In a few places the West Temple can be seen in the distance. The huge boulders on the west side of the roadway near here fell from the Springdale ledge and the rubble cap. Some have fallen within the past few decades.

The unconformable contact between the upper member of the Chinle Formation (gray and purple shale) and the Dinosaur Canyon Member of the Moenave (brownish red) shows through the talus in a few places on the west side of the road between here and the South Campground entrance. The Chinle becomes more evident as you proceed into Springdale.

To the east the canyon wall consists of slopes (Dinosaur Canyon Member and Kayenta) and cliffs (Springdale Member and Navajo). The flat bottom of the canyon here is due partly to alluvial infilling caused by Pleistocene and Holocene (?) damming downstream (by lava and slump blocks) and to the accelerated rate of breakdown of the canyon walls caused by slump following exposure of the slippery Chinle shales.

Arch on Bridge Mountain.

V. L. JACKSON

Zion Canyon Scenic Drive

V. L. JACKSON

Emerald Pools waterfalls.

Canyon Junction:

DISTANCES UPCANYON		DISTANCES DOWNCANYON	
0.0 km	**(0.0 mi)**	10.6 km	**(6.6 mi)**

See distances west to east km 2.6 (mile 1.6) of Zion — Mt. Carmel Highway log.

Sentinel Slide area pulloff:

1.1 km	**(0.7 mi)**	9.5 km	**(5.9 mi)**

On the west side of the river, left as you go upstream, contorted and broken beds of Kayenta shale, siltstone and sandstone outcrop amidst an accumulation of slide debris. Here and there at the road and river level the nearly flat-lying Springdale Sandstone bedrock ledge shows through. Capping the bench is Navajo Sandstone rubble, consisting of huge blocks in some places. The bench is made up mainly of slump-block and slide material that moved into the canyon from a location near the face of the Sentinel, creating a

lake upstream. This occurred about 4,000 years ago, based on a radiocarbon date on plant carbon in the lake sediments.

In places along the water's edge on the east bank, ripple marked sandstone of the Springdale Member can be seen. Ripple marks can also be seen in the sand that lines the bed of the Virgin River here, but they are shaped differently than the fossil ripple marks. The streams of Springdale time flowed more slowly than the Virgin.

Across the river the Springdale ledge has been beautifully sculptured by flowing surface water and the fragmenting effect of salt crystallization. The result is an excellent example of cavernous weathering.

Court of the Patriarchs:

2.7 km	**(1.7 mi)**	7.9 km	**(4.9 mi)**

From the parking area on the right you can walk to a nearby overlook for an outstanding view into Birch Creek Canyon, also known as the Court of the Patriarchs. Navajo Sandstone cliffs dominate the scene. The slope at the base of the Navajo is formed on the Kayenta Formation, broken by a tongue of cross-bedded Navajo that forms a low cliff near river level.

At the overlook you are standing on a thin veneer of stream and slump deposits that cover gray lake clays. The clays were deposited in the lake that backed up behind the Sentinel slump and slide mass immediately south of Birch Creek. Sentinel Lake sediments have been about half removed by the river since the dam was breached about 3,600 ± 400 years ago, but enough remains to give the floor of the canyon a flat bottom between here and Angels Landing.

If you walk to the river from here and cross the footbridge at Birch Creek you will have an excellent view of slide debris overlain by river deposits downstream and lake clays upstream.

Pulloff on left:

3.2 km   **(2.0 mi)**   *7.4 km*   **(4.6 mi)**

River terraces developed on lake and stream deposits can be seen by walking to the riverbank from here. In the course of the past few centuries the meandering channel has left its imprint at three successive levels.

Stream deposits may be seen overlying lake clays in the exposure on the opposite bank. Downcutting has been temporarily stopped in this section by the construction of a concrete dam at Birch Creek. The dam protects a major pipeline carrying culinary water for Park use.

Lodge Entrance and
Emerald Pools Trailhead:

4.5 km   **(2.8 mi)**   *6.1 km*   **(3.8 mi)**

On the left is the parking area for the Emerald Pools Trail. This trail enters Heaps Canyon, where it takes you beneath two waterfalls which plunge over a Navajo Sandstone tongue. Seepage at the base of the sandstone there leaves white deposits of sodium bicarbonate on the rock. An outstanding exposure of the Sentinel Lake clay is seen in the short gully located about 15 m (50 feet) north of the river footbridge.

Middle Emerald Pool.

ROY GIVEN

V. L. JACKSON

The Pulpit, Temple of Sinawava.

Grotto Picnic Area and West Rim Trailhead:

5.6 km	(3.5 mi)	5.0 km	(3.1 mi)

This is the takeoff point for the West Rim Trail for those hardy souls who would rather hike up to Lava Point than down from there into the canyon. The north face of Cathedral Mountain displays excellent checkerboarding above Scout Lookout. Kayenta sediments are largely blanketed by talus in this area, but the tongue of Navajo Sandstone may be inspected where it outcrops just above the picnic area. It contains thin limestones at its top in this area.

About 160 m (0.1 mile) upcanyon from here cross-bedding may be seen in the Navajo tongue at the right side of the roadway.

Pulloff on left:

6.6 km	(4.1 mi)	4.0 km	(2.5 mi)

Across the main canyon is narrow Refrigerator Canyon through which the West Rim Trail passes on its way to Scout Lookout. The mouth of Refrigerator Canyon is about 100 m (350 feet) above the base of the Navajo, therefore it is called a "hanging" canyon. This has nothing to do with its having been scoured by ice as were the hanging valleys in Yosemite. The hanging canyons (such as Hidden Canyon) have been left high (and frequently dry) because their development has been retarded as tributaries of the larger canyons (such as Echo Canyon) have "pirated" their watersheds, leaving less and less water to them. Even the pirate canyons such as Echo Canyon have had their watersheds pirated by other larger canyons such as the tributary canyons of Clear Creek, leaving them with underdeveloped upper portions characterized by waterfalls.

A large sandy bank may be seen near the river below the mouth of Refrigerator Canyon. It is a delta deposit, formed in Sentinel Lake at times when the stream flowed from the side canyon.

Weeping Rock and East Rim Trailhead:

7.7 km	(4.8 mi)	2.9 km	(1.8 mi)

Zion Canyon's great meander is formed as the river winds around Angels Landing and The Organ. Several other meanders are found farther upcanyon in the Narrows. The feature that characterizes their existence is the presence in each case of a major side canyon. It appears that they have developed in response to more rapid canyon widening on the side where the mouth of the tributary canyon is located. They are not, then, true intrenched meanders "let down" from a previous higher erosional surface.

Weeping Rock Spring is located below the mouths of two hanging canyons: Echo Canyon and an unnamed one that heads up just east of Observation Point. These upland drainages serve to collect surface water runoff, concentrating groundwater within the Navajo aquifer and supporting the spring. A smaller spring, a few hundred meters to the south, lies below the mouth of Hidden Canyon. Weeping Rock Spring and others in the canyon are rather highly alkaline and deposits of calcareous tufa (limestone) are forming on the wet sandstone.

The alkaline water and abundant aquatic algae make the stream at Weeping Rock an excellent habitat for the freshwater snail, *Physa virgata*. It appears that this snail is a very recent colonist here because it was not reported by naturalists in the 1930s.

The East Rim Trail starts here. There is a side trail into Hidden Canyon (another hanging canyon). The trail to Observation Point provides some excellent views of slump structures formed before lithification in the silty portion of the Temple Cap Formation. The East Rim Trail tops out on the Navajo just at the point where the Echo Canyon Fault cuts across on a north-northwest heading. There are good examples of checkerboarding on the north face of Cable Mountain.

Great White Throne turnout, downcanyon traffic only:

No exit	2.1 km	*(1.3 mi)*

This stop provides unsurpassed views of The Great White Throne and the north face of Angels Landing. The upper, white Navajo gives the dominant impression on the former while the redder lower portion of the Navajo predominates on the sheer wall of Angels Landing.

Non-vertical jointing in the Navajo ridge between Angels Landing and The Organ (the monolith jutting out toward Weeping Rock) suggests that The Organ may be slowly moving toward the river.

The Great White Throne seen from the Temple of Sinawava.

V. L. JACKSON

Temple of Sinawava and Narrows Trailhead:

10.6 km	*(6.6 mi)*	0.0 km	*(0.0 mi)*

At this point Zion Canyon narrows down appreciably, because this is effectively the base of the Navajo Sandstone. Yet the river is currently not cutting bedrock here as it is at the beginning of the narrow portions of other canyons in the Park because the damming and alluviation effects of the Sentinel slump and slide are felt well upstream from the highest lake sediments. It will be many years before the river reaches its previous base level here.

The Gateway to the Narrows Trail begins here. It parallels the river on the east bank for 1.6 km (1 mile) until the canyon becomes so narrow that hikers must take to the water. This is a good place to see desert varnish high on the sandstone walls. It glistens bluish-black in the sunlight.

The trail passes beneath an area of extensive water seepage from the sandstone, water that supports a fabulous "hanging garden" community of plants and animals. As at Weeping Rock the water is depositing tufa, but there is a different population of snails here. They are *Physa zionis*, a snail found, as far as we know, only on the vertical walls in this canyon.

Across the river convoluted bedding is seen in the Navajo. Roughly 60 m (200 feet) above river level an approximately 0.5 m (1.5 feet) thick stratum of dolomite is visible. These features point to the influence of water during deposition of the lower part of the formation.

If you hike farther upstream past the end of the trail you will come to places where the sandstone at hand level seems to have been polished like glass by rushing water during floods. A closer look reveals that the "polish" is actually a smooth coating of tufa deposited by the turbulent river.

State Route 9 and Kolob Road to Lava Point

South Entrance:

DISTANCES FROM SOUTH ENTRANCE		DISTANCES FROM LAVA POINT	
0.0 km	*(0.0 mi)*	62.5 km	*(38.8 mi)*

See km (mile) 0.0 of Zion — Mt. Carmel Highway log. Through Springdale many good views of the upper Chinle are available in the washes to the north.

Petrified Forest Road:

6.1 km	*(3.8 mi)*	56.4 km	*(35.0 mi)*

Here a rocky road climbs the broken-down Shinarump ledge providing access across private land to the Park boundary. The area behind the boundary gate is closed to all vehicles, so one must be prepared to hike into the Petrified Forest area. The walk is well worth it, however the easiest access is via Huber Wash leading north from the first bridge west of Rockville.

At about 6.0 km (3.7 miles) you will see Pleistocene conglomerate unconformably overlying Moenkopi shale. At 6.2 km (3.85 miles) a high-angle reverse fault cuts through the Shinarump ledge above the highway.

Grafton turnoff:

8.0 km	*(5.0 mi)*	54.5 km	*(33.8 mi)*

You can cross the Virgin River here to gain access to Grafton, a ghost town several kilometers to the west. The river is still above an earlier grade level there and is cutting into cemented gravels just west of Grafton. This may be the result of tipping sometime after 0.5 million years before present.

View of Crater Hill:

11.1 km	*(6.9 mi)*	51.4 km	*(31.9 mi)*

On the horizon straight ahead is a conical mound called Crater Hill, a cinder cone marking the site of an extinct volcano. Its age is somewhat less than about 0.5 million years, the date determined by Winnett and Sutter for one of the oldest flows associated with the volcano.

Coalpits Wash:

12.7 km	*(7.9 mi)*	49.8 km	*(30.9 mi)*

If you park well off the highway on the north side, you can hike into the Park along Coalpits Wash. This is the lowest point in the Park at about 1,100 m (3,600 feet). The wash is usually dry, so you may be surprised to see a few tiny fish in some of the pools farther upstream. Pleistocene river gravels cap slightly older lake deposits here, but in general it is very difficult to distinguish between the lake beds and Moenkopi floodplain deposits of Triassic age. The lake deposits were laid down behind a dam produced when the Crater Hill lava flows blocked the Virgin River. The present channel of the Virgin has developed along the southern margin of the flow.

View of Pine Valley Mountain:

17.7 km	*(11.0 mi)*	44.8 km	*(27.8 mi)*

One of several excellent views of Pine Valley Mountain on the western horizon is available here. Pine Valley Mountain is an enormous body of igneous rock, monzonite and latite, emplaced and extruded through the early Tertiary sediments north of St. George.

Dalton Wash Road:

21.9 km	*(13.6 mi)*	40.6 km	*(25.2 mi)*

The small road to the right leads to the Park boundary in the Crater Hill area and the headwaters of Coalpits Wash through lava-marginal

Crater Hill.

Chinle Formation near Rockville, Utah.

Dalton Wash. In places near the boundary it becomes almost a four-wheel-drive road.

Virgin and junction with Kolob Reservoir Road:

24.2 km	(15.0 mi)	38.3 km	(23.8 mi)

The blacktop road to the right leads north into the Kolob Terrace area, crosses the midsection of the Park and re-enters the Park near Lava Point.

Virgin Oil Field:

27.4 km	(17.0 mi)	35.1 km	(21.8 mi)

Production here is from the Timpoweap Member of the Moenkopi at a depth of only a few hundred meters. The structure is located less than 3 km (2 miles) west of the Cougar Mountain graben, but it is believed to be unassociated with that feature. Reservoir conditions may be represented by the structures that can be seen in the Timpoweap at the Scenic Overlook of the Virgin River Gorge between Virgin and La Verkin.

The basalt capping the mesa east of the field has been dated at 1.0 m.y. by Myron Best of Brigham Young University.

Basalt on stream gravels:

29.3 km	(18.2 mi)	33.2 km	(20.6 mi)

The North Creek volcanic flows are estimated to lie in the range of from less than 1 m.y. to approximately a quarter million years before present. This basalt issued from vents in Cave Valley and perhaps Lee Valley and seriously interrupted the development of the North Creek drainage. In places upstream within the Park lava damming produced sizeable lakes.

Inverted Valley:

32.8 km	(20.4 mi)	29.7 km	(18.4 mi)

Lava marginal stream dissection has left the original basalt-filled stream channel high and dry. The road climbs onto this inverted valley providing an appealing view of the Sunset Canyon Ranch, located on North Creek at the Park boundary.

Park boundary:

35.6 km	(22.1 mi)	26.9 km	(16.7 mi)

Here and there one can see ahead through the pinyon and juniper into the area of the confluence of the Left and Right Forks of North Creek. Cougar Mountain, a block of Navajo Sandstone in the Cougar Mountain graben, looms to the right. The road here is about level with the top of the Shinarump.

Junction with Smith Mesa Road:

37.7 km	*(23.4 mi)*	*24.8 km*	*(15.4 mi)*

The left fork will take you to Smith Mesa and Hurricane Mesa and eventually after opening and closing many cattle gates back down to State Route 9 near Virgin. This junction lies slightly east of the West Cougar Mountain Fault, which can be plainly seen by following the Smith Mesa Road a short distance.

Parking area for hikers:

38.6 km	*(24.0 mi)*	*23.9 km*	*(14.8 mi)*

One gains access into the canyon of the Left Fork of North Creek here. If you have been there you will understand why the National Park Service issues backcountry permits only after a thorough briefing on routes and conditions. It is rugged, but incredibly beautiful, country.

Those who hike about two miles up the Left Fork will see a slab of Kayenta Sandstone on the streambank containing numerous large dinosaur footprints (see Figure 71).

Cave Valley:

41.9 km	*(26.0 mi)*	*20.6 km*	*(12.8 mi)*

Cave Valley contains many parcels of private land within the Park boundary, so hiking access can be a problem in places. A volcanic vent marked by red cinders has been excavated on the west side of the road. Straight ahead the gray mound on the horizon is Spendlove Knoll, a cinder cone marking the final stages of the volcanic activity that filled this valley and North Creek with lava about 0.26 m.y. ago. At km 42.5 (mile 26.4) the road exits the Park.

Hop Valley Road:

45.4 km	*(28.2 mi)*	*17.1 km*	*(10.6 mi)*

The dirt road to the left leads a few hundred meters to a gate where one gains access across private land to the Hop Valley Trail.

East Cougar Mountain Fault (elevation 1,980 m, 6,500 feet):

47.2 km	*(29.3 mi)*	*15.3 km*	*(9.5 mi)*

You are now back inside the Park. The fault trace, forming the east margin of the Cougar Mountain graben, passes north-northwestward from Lee Valley into Hop Valley between Spendlove Knoll (on the right) and Firepit Knoll (on the left). One gets the impression that these volcanoes are related to the fault. The West Temple and Towers of the Virgin appear in the distance to the south, the Finger Canyons can be seen to the north.

View of Malony Hill:

48.1 km	*(29.9 mi)*	*14.4 km*	*(8.9 mi)*

The lava capping the highest mesa straight ahead has been dated at about 1.4 m.y. by Myron

Firepit Knoll.

Best of Brigham Young University. The lower flows are about half as old and about the same age as the basalt at Lava Point (see km 62.5, mile 38.8).

Overlook:

51.5 km	*(32.6 mi)*	*11.0 km*	*(6.2 mi)*

Here at about 2,190 m (7,200 feet) elevation you have a view of the lower Kolob Terrace, the St. George basin and on most days as far as the Virgin Mountains near Littlefield, Arizona, about 95 km (60 miles) to the southwest.

Head of "Black Canyon":

54.6 km	*(33.9 mi)*	7.9 km	*(4.9 mi)*

The fractured upper contact of the Navajo Sandstone can be seen along the right side of the road. The Temple Cap Formation appears on the lower slope of the hillside straight ahead.

Park boundary:

56.2 km	*(34.9 mi)*	6.3 km	*(3.9 mi)*

The lower limestone member of the Carmel Formation is well exposed here. There are karst features in this area, including the "sinks" on the left side of the road.

Lava Point Road junction:

59.6 km	*(37.0 mi)*	2.9 km	*(1.8 mi)*

As you turn right here to re-enter the Park, Home Valley Knoll is seen about 0.8 km (0.5 mile) away to the right. It is another extinct volcano, probably the one responsible for the extensive flows over which you have been driving since leaving "Black Canyon". The hill behind you to the north is the remaining part of an older volcano that probably produced the higher 1.4 million year old flows. In the far distance on your left the pink cliffs of the early Tertiary (Paleocene?) Cedar Breaks Formation (the Red Claron member) are visible.

View from Lava Point.

Park boundary:

61.0 km	*(37.9 mi)*	1.5 km	*(0.9 mi)*

The road crosses Blue Creek, the headwaters of Wildcat Canyon. At the crest of the hill 0.2 km (0.1 mile) ahead the road to the left leads 2.2 km (1.4 miles) to the head of the West Rim Trail. The right fork takes you to Lava Point.

Lava Point:

62.5 km	*(38.8 mi)*	0.0 km	*(0.0 mi)*

At the overlook by the fire lookout station you can see approximately 110 km (70 miles) to Mt. Trumbull (south) and the Kaibab Plateau (south-east) on most days. The near view is of the headward portions of Kolob Creek, Goose Creek and Wildcat canyons and the Horse Pasture Plateau. The Horse Pasture Plateau and other parts of the "terrace" at that elevation are capped by the buff and gray limestone member of the Carmel Formation of mid-Jurassic age. The canyons are cut into the underlying Navajo Sandstone.

The basalt at Lava Point has been dated at 0.7 m.y. by Myron Best, using the potassium-argon method. It is about half as old as the flow that caps the mesa above "Black Canyon" and roughly twice as old as the North Creek flows. The source of the Lava Point basalt is thought to have been at Home Valley Knoll, about 1.6 km (1 mile) to the west. Home Valley Knoll lies on the trace of the Wildcat Canyon Fault, though the fault is hidden by volcanic rock north of the Wildcat Canyon Trail.

Road to Kolob Canyons, Taylor Creek Area

South Entrance:

DISTANCES TO		DISTANCES FROM	
0.0 km	*(0.0 mi)*	75.2 km	*(46.7 mi)*

See State Route 9 and Kolob Road to Lava Point log for points of interest between the South Entrance and the town of Virgin.

Virgin and junction with Kolob Reservoir Road:

24.2 km	*(15.0 mi)*	51.0 km	*(31.7 mi)*

Continue straight ahead on State Route 9. The Virgin Limestone Member of the Moenkopi Formation outcrops 30 m (100 feet) or so above the town. It is yellowish-tan in color, forms a low ledge and is fairly fossiliferous.

As you continue westward Hurricane Mesa dominates the skyline on your right. Several water towers can be seen on top, part of a military test facility. Virtually the entire section of the Moen-kopi Formation, except the lowest member, the Timpoweap Limestone, can be seen on the face of the mesa. The top is capped by the Shinarump Conglomerate.

Hurricane Mesa Road:

26.4 km	*(16.4 mi)*	48.8 km	*(30.3 mi)*

The road to the right leads to the top of Hurricane Mesa. The drive up closely resembles flying. Petrified logs are exposed in the Shinarump at the top. As elsewhere in this area, the "wood" is decidedly drab in color.

Road to the Cracks:

29.3 km	*(18.2 mi)*	45.9 km	*(28.5 mi)*

Most local residents in years past knew about this unusual place. If you take the dirt road to the left to its end you will very abruptly come to a vertical dropoff into the Virgin River Gorge, cut into the Timpoweap and Kaibab Limestones. The bedrock near the edge is broken into myriad deep cracks, presumably by collapse following undermining by water.

The Timpoweap here exhibits gentle fold structures which do not continue downward into the Kaibab. It is thought that they were formed by slump on a gently sloping sea floor while the sediments were still soft.

Road to Scenic View:

30.4 km	*(18.9 mi)*	44.8 km	*(27.8 mi)*

This side road to the left also ends abruptly, so be ready to stop just before the Virgin River Gorge comes into view.

Starting down the escarpment of the Hurricane Fault:

31.0 km	*(19.3 mi)*	44.2 km	*(27.4 mi)*

The Hurricane Fault is actually a series of subparallel faults, and you will cross several of them in the next two kilometers. Slickensides are evident in places showing that movement was in an up and down direction. The west block has dropped relative to the east, and the movement amounted to about 1,200 m (4,000 feet) over the past several million years or so. This is a potential earthquake zone.

The view to the northwest includes the south end of Black Ridge, which is the lava-capped eastern limb of the Kanarra Fold. The Taylor Creek Thrust Zone of Lovejoy (1964) and Kurie (1966) lies just east of the crest of the ridge. The fold is cut along its axis here by the younger portion of the Hurricane Fault.

Junction:

35.2 km	**(21.9 mi)**	40.0 km	**(24.8 mi)**

This is La Verkin. Turn right here.

Junction:

44.8 km	**(27.8 mi)**	30.4 km	**(18.9 mi)**

Turn right onto Interstate 15 northbound.

View of Horse Ranch Mountain:

49.3 km	**(30.6 mi)**	25.9 km	**(16.1 mi)**

Straight ahead in the distance you can see Horse Ranch Mountain, 2,664 m (8,740 feet), the highest point in the Park.

Exit to Kolob Canyons:

66.0 km	**(41.0 mi)**	9.2 km	**(5.7 mi)**

Turn right here to re-enter the Park for a 9.2 km (5.7 mile) drive into some of the finest scenery on Earth.

Your first pulloff 0.5 km (0.33 mile) ahead lies almost exactly on the trace of the Hurricane Fault, here buried beneath recent alluvium. The escarpment of the fault has been eroded back somewhat here and consists of horizontal and west-dipping blocks of Timpoweap Limestone

Kolob Canyons area.

blanketed by rose-colored Moenkopi shales. About 0.4 km (0.25 mile) to the south, just outside the boundary, are several exploratory mine drifts in the Kaibab and Timpoweap Limestones. They were excavated during the uranium boom of the 1950's.

Kolob Canyons Visitor Center:

66.5 km	**(41.3 mi)**	8.7 km	**(5.4 mi)**

A gate just beyond here may be temporarily closed from late fall to early spring due to recent snow or rockfalls which have not been removed. It is best to check here or at the Zion Canyon Visitor Center for current conditions.

Pulloff on left:

68.6 km	**(42.6 mi)**	6.6 km	**(4.1 mi)**

Taylor Creek has cut through a series of north-south ridges. The ridges are called cuestas, formed by resistant layers of east-dipping sedimentary rock on the eastern limb of the Kanarra Fold. The westernmost cuesta is formed on the resistant Virgin Member of the Moenkopi Formation. Next is a ridge capped by Shinarump Conglomerate. Then one held up by the Springdale Member of the Moenave. Then because of overthrusting, *another* Springdale-capped cuesta! The north-south valleys consist of the easily eroded shales and siltstones of the respective formations. The topography is reminiscent of the Ridge and Valley Province of the Appalachians in Pennsylvania and West Virginia.

Straight ahead you see Horse Ranch Mountain with excellent exposure of Navajo Sandstone, the Carmel Formation, Dakota Sandstone and small outcrops of Pleistocene basalt. The Temple Cap is so thin as to be essentially absent, but otherwise the entire geological cross section of the Park can be seen in this area because the Kanarra Fold brings the lower rocks into view.

If you look carefully you may see several north-south, near vertical normal faults in road cuts.

Pulloff on left:

69.7 km	*(43.3 mi)*	*5.5 km*	*(3.4 mi)*

At this point you are on a level with the Shinarump Conglomerate, the lowest member of the Triassic Chinle Formation.

Pulloff on right:

70.5 km	*(43.8 mi)*	*4.7 km*	*(2.9 mi)*

The road has now turned southeastward along the South Fork of Taylor Creek. The view to the north and south from here shows the *two* Springdale-topped cuestas mentioned earlier. This is because the rocks on the east have been thrust over the rocks to the west along the Taylor Creek Thrust Zone. Farther west in Utah and Nevada the direction of thrusting was exactly the opposite (western block over eastern).

Water-gap:

71.3 km	*(44.3 mi)*	*3.9 km*	*(2.4 mi)*

This narrow part of the South Fork drainage, where the stream has cut through the Springdale ledge, was blocked by a slide from the north about 3,600 years before present (based on carbon-14 dating of an exhumed pine tree). A few hundred meters ahead are two pulloffs on the right from which you can see the lake sediments which accumulated behind the slide dam. An even better view of the lake deposits can be had by crossing the roadway and looking up the canyon of the South Fork. The lake sediments consist of alternating layers of white sand and thin black organic clays.

About 0.8 km (0.5 mile) upcanyon you will see another slide mass draped across the mouth of the narrow part of the canyon of the South Fork. A seasonal pond still forms behind that dam, although the pond basin is nearly filled with sediment, and it will probably not be long before the dam is breached.

The brick-red and brown strata of the Kayenta Formation are exceptionally well exposed alongside the road to the south, and the Navajo Sandstone is at its best in this area, being red throughout its entire thickness.

Lee Pass:

72.8 km	*(45.2 mi)*	*2.4 km*	*(1.5 mi)*

This is the trailhead for La Verkin Creek Trail. The trail drops down into Timber Creek to the south, then turns eastward along La Verkin Creek. A spur trail from La Verkin Creek leads to Kolob Arch, the largest freestanding arch known on Earth. The span has been measured at 94 m (310 feet).

Here at Lee Pass you have returned to the contact between the Kayenta and the Springdale Sandstone (respectively on the east and west sides of the road). The road now traverses the eastward dipslope of the Kanarra Fold where falling rocks are a constant nuisance.

Pulloff on left:

74.7 km	*(46.4 mi)*	*0.5 km*	*(0.3 mi)*

Moenave rocks on the upper plate of the Taylor Creek Thrust have been folded into a vertical attitude in the roadcut to the right.

Slide dam, South Fork of Taylor Creek.

Overlook and end of Kolob Canyons Road:

75.2 km	*(46.7 mi)*	0.0 km	*(0.0 mi)*

It is easy to see why the canyons to the east have been called the Finger Canyons. They have been formed along joints and in some cases tear faults developed in the overthrust plate of the Taylor Creek Thrust. The thrust zone passes almost exactly through the parking area here, although it is hidden by mudflow and slide debris, and divides the two Springdale ledges on the west side of the crest of the ridge to the north. To the south the faults are traced with some difficulty to the next gully. Thereafter it is more difficult to find them because the Springdale Sandstone has been severely shattered by gravity-sliding toward the east.

V. L. JACKSON

Finger Canyons of the Kolob.

Time Scales
APPENDIX

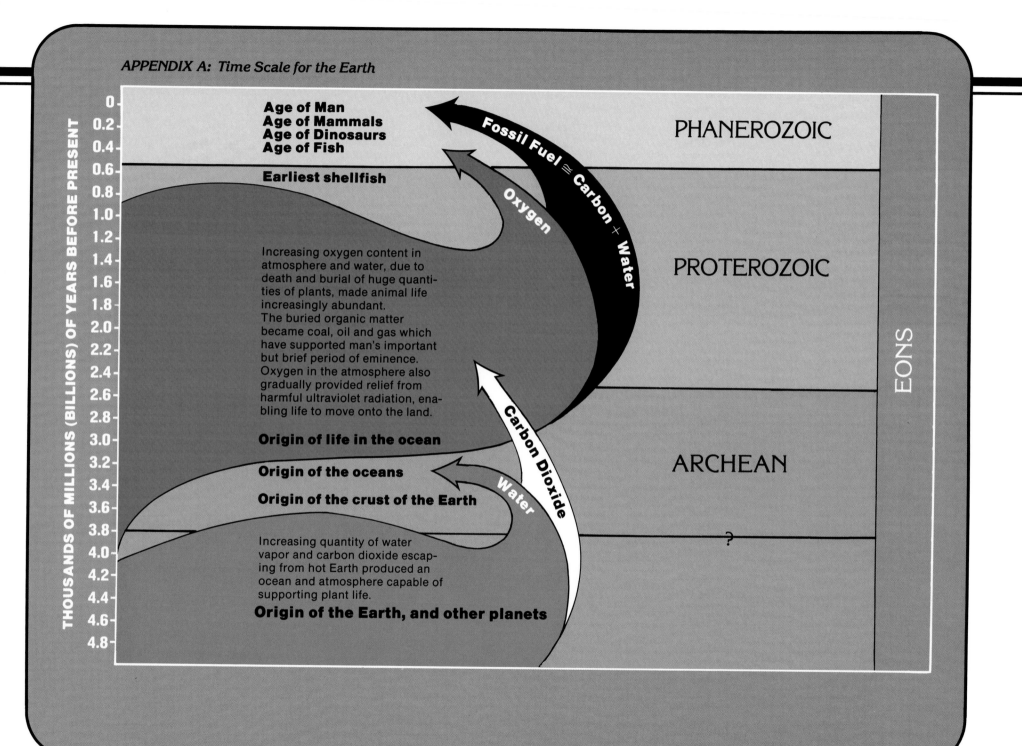

APPENDIX A: *Time Scale for the Earth*

THOUSANDS OF MILLIONS (BILLIONS) OF YEARS BEFORE PRESENT

0
0.2
0.4
0.6
0.8
1.0
1.2
1.4
1.6
1.8
2.0
2.2
2.4
2.6
2.8
3.0
3.2
3.4
3.6
3.8
4.0
4.2
4.4
4.6
4.8

Age of Man
Age of Mammals
Age of Dinosaurs
Age of Fish

Earliest shellfish

Increasing oxygen content in atmosphere and water, due to death and burial of huge quantities of plants, made animal life increasingly abundant.
The buried organic matter became coal, oil and gas which have supported man's important but brief period of eminence. Oxygen in the atmosphere also gradually provided relief from harmful ultraviolet radiation, enabling life to move onto the land.

Origin of life in the ocean

Origin of the oceans

Origin of the crust of the Earth

Increasing quantity of water vapor and carbon dioxide escaping from hot Earth produced an ocean and atmosphere capable of supporting plant life.

Origin of the Earth, and other planets

Fossil Fuel ≅ Carbon + Water

Oxygen

Carbon Dioxide

Water

PHANEROZOIC

PROTEROZOIC

ARCHEAN

?

EONS

APPENDIX B: *Geologic Time Scale and Geologic Columns for Zion National Park*

ERAS	PERIODS	EPOCHS	EVENTS	FORMATIONS
Cenozoic	Quaternary	Recent (10,000 yrs)	Sentinel Lake	Virgin River deposits
		Pleistocene	Crater Hill volcanics / Lava Point volcanics	Coalpits Formation
		Pliocene		
		Miocene	Tipping of Markagunt Plateau & normal faulting (?) / Origin of Man	
	Tertiary	Oligocene	Pine Valley Mountain volcanics / Taylor Creek Thrust (?)	
		Eocene	Regional uplift & development of joints (?)	
		Paleocene	Extinction of dinosaurs, flowering of mammals	
Mesozoic	Cretaceous	Late		Dakota Formation
		Early	Stream deposition / Kanarra Fold (?)	
	Jurassic	Late		Carmel Formation / Temple Cap Formation / Navajo Formation / Kayenta Formation (?) / Moenave Formation
		Middle	Nearshore marine / Coastal desert	
		Early	Streams & lakes	
	Triassic	Late	Swamps, lakes & rivers	Chinle Formation
		Middle	Coastal deltas	
		Early	Breakup of Pangaea	Moenkopi Formation
Paleozoic	Permian	Late	Nearshore marine	Kaibab Formation
			Carboniferous, Devonian, Silurian, Ordovician, Cambrian, etc.	Older sediments are not exposed in Zion

MILLIONS OF YEARS BEFORE PRESENT

0, 20, 40, 60, 80, 100, 120, 140, 160, 180, 200, 220, 240, 260, 280

Chronology after *Decade of North American Geology GSA*

APPENDIX C: Timescale of Quaternary events in Zion, based on potassium-argon dates

MILLIONS OF YEARS BEFORE PRESENT

EPOCHS	EVENTS		FORMATIONS
	Slide lakes		Lake and river deposits
	Hurricane Fault displacement	Spendlove Knoll and Firepit Knoll volcanoes	Trail Canyon Lake deposits
	Crater Hill volcano		Coalpits Lake deposits
	Home Valley Knoll volcano		Lava Point lavas
		Wildcat Canyon Fault	
			Older North Creek lavas
	Cougar Mountain faults	Beartrap Fault	Malony Hill lavas

Epochs (vertical axis left): Pleistocene, Pliocene

Scale: 0, 0.5, 1.0, 1.5, 2.0

APPENDIX D: Timescale for Recent events in Zion: based on radiocarbon dating

YEARS BEFORE PRESENT

Scale: 0, 1,000, 2,000, 3,000, 4,000, 5,000

- 670 ±200 Hop Valley Lake nearly full

ca 1,500 Hop Valley slide dam

- 2,880 ±200 Paria Lake nearly full
- 3,600 ±400 Sentinel Lake drained
- 3,610 ±300 Paria Lake dam

ca 4,000 Sentinel slump & slide dam

GLOSSARY

A

AEOLIAN - Pertaining to deposition by the wind.

ALKALINE - Used in reference to water containing large quantities of dissolved carbonate. When the carbonate is precipitated, it is usually as calcium carbonate.

ALLUVIUM - The sedimentary deposits of rivers and streams.

AMMONITE - One of a now extinct group of marine coiled mollusks, similar to the nautilus. Ammonites underwent such rapid evolution and were so widely distributed in the marine environment that they are extremely useful as diagnostic fossils in dating marine sediments.

ANDESITE - A volcanic rock consisting mainly of the feldspar mineral andesine and one or more dark, ferromagnesian minerals like pyroxene, hornblende or biotite.

ANHYDRITE - A mineral, calcium sulfate, which precipitates from highly saline seawater.

ANTICLINE - A fold formed by lateral compression in layered rocks that appears convex-upward when viewed in cross section. Anticlines are the structures sought by oil companies because they tend to trap and accumulate droplets of oil that move with water in some aquifers.

AQUICLUDE - A stratum that is essentially impermeable to the flow of groundwater, like clay.

AQUIFER - A permeable zone located in the rock or subsoil that contains flowing groundwater. The water flows slowly in the pores of the aquifer and usually does not constitute an "underground river."

ARCH - A natural arch-shaped rock structure formed primarily by rockfall on steep bedrock exposures. Arches may be freestanding, where one may walk beneath them from one side to the other, or "blind", where

they are formed in *bas-relief* on a cliff face. Arch formation is discussed on page 37.

B

BASALT - A fine-grained, dark-colored volcanic rock, formed from cooled lava, that contains tiny crystals of calcium and magnesium-rich minerals (like plagioclase feldspar and pyroxene) and perhaps some olivine crystals. Basalt often contains glass, rock that has been quenched so rapidly that it has not crystallized.

BASE LEVEL - The level at which a stream gradient becomes zero and below which it cannot erode, e.g. lake or sea level.

BEDDING - Essentially synonymous with layering. A bed is a sedimentary layer more than 1 cm thick.

BEDROCK - The solid rock of the Earth's crust as distinct from the mantling material such as soil, talus, and other unconsolidated deposits.

BENTONITE - A clay produced by the weathering of volcanic ash. It swells on contact with water and shrinks on drying.

BRACHIOPOD - An individual of the phylum of marine bivalves which resemble pelecypods, except that the two valves (shells) are dissimilar.

BRECCIA - Rock consisting of broken rock fragments cemented (or welded) together.

BRYOZOAN - An individual of a phylum of colonial, aquatic animals that superficially resemble plants. Sea fans are bryozoans.

C

CANYON - A steep-walled gorge. A deep valley that has a cross section like a V or U or even ⊔.

CARBONATE - An ion, that is, part of a molecule, composed of one carbon atom and three oxygen atoms. The electrical charge of the carbon (+4) is not balanced by the

charges of the oxygen (altogether -6); therefore the ion bears a charge of -2. Carbonate is written as CO_3^{-2}.

CARBON-14 - See radiocarbon

CAVERNOUS WEATHERING - Weathering, often accompanied by fragmentation due to crystallization of salts in a dry environment, that produces cavities in rock ledges and boulders. Such cavities are often floored with loose weathered debris, and on several occasions I have slept very comfortably in such caves developed in sandstone.

CENOZOIC - The latest era of geologic time.

CHECKERBOARDING - A rectilinear groove pattern formed on the surface of planar cross-bedded sandstone in combination with fracturing caused by surficial expansion and contraction. See page 32 of the text.

CINDER CONE - A rounded conical mound of cinders formed over some volcanic vents. A cinder

cone often has a depression at the top.

CLAST - An individual piece of sediment, e.g. a rock or a sand grain that acts as a unit in the depositional environment.

CLAY - Clay means at least two things. It is used to designate small sedimentary particles smaller than 0.004 millimeter in diameter. It also means a class of minerals, like hydrous aluminum silicates, which become very sticky when wet. The definitions merge because usually when mineral particles are ground down to small size they are readily altered chemically to clay minerals.

CLAYSTONE - Soft sedimentary rock consisting of clay-size particles, which does not split into laminae, but which breaks into blocks or irregular masses.

COLORADO PLATEAU - A geological province in the western United States which is characterized by relatively flat-lying Paleozoic, Mesozoic and Cenozoic sedimentary rocks, indicating that it has been relatively unaffected by deformation for several hundred million years. It includes part of Utah, Arizona, Colorado and New Mexico.

CONCRETION-A rounded rock mass, often with concentric layers around a nucleus.

CONGLOMERATE-A sedimentary rock consisting of gravel and sand cemented with calcite, silica or iron oxides.

CONSEQUENT DRAINAGE-A stream drainage system developed on an area of the Earth's surface which is primarily shaped by the structural attitude of the bedrock. For example, on a terrain developed on gently dipping strata the streams will tend to flow in the direction of dip under the influence of gravity. The stream pattern is a *consequence* of the direction of dip.

CONTACT-The plane of juxtaposition between two rock units, usually between two formations.

On a geologic map this plane is expressed as a line of contact where it intersects the surface of the ground.

CONTINENTAL SHELF-The gently sloping submarine margin of a continent.

CONVOLUTED BEDDING-Twisted and folded layering in sediments produced when the sediments are still soft, that is, shortly after deposition.

CRETACEOUS-The last period of geologic time in the Mesozoic era, spanning the interval from 144 to 66 million years before present.

CRINOID-A marine animal of the phylum *Echinodermata* which consists of a long stalk attached to the sea bottom and a flower-like head. The pieces of the segmented stalk resemble buttons.

CROSS-STRATIFICATION OR CROSS-BEDDING-Sedimentary layers separated by inclined bedding planes which are non-horizontal

because they were originally deposited on a slope like the lee side of a dune.

CRUST-The Earth's outermost layer of rock. It consists of basalt about 6 km (4 miles) thick with a thin skin of sediments beneath the ocean basins. More silica-rich rock, like granite, with thick deposits of sediments and large amounts of metamorphic rock totaling 30 to 70 km (19 to 44 miles) thick make up the continental crust.

CUESTA-A ridge formed along the outcrop of a dipping rock stratum which is more resistant to erosion than the adjacent layers.

D

DEFORMATION-The process by which a body like the Earth's crust becomes wrinkled, faulted or tipped.

DELTA-A triangular sedimentary body which forms where a stream flows into a quiet body of water, such as the sea or a lake.

DEPOSITION-The process of being dropped or laid down.

DESERT VARNISH-A shiny hard black clay incrustation found on rock surfaces in desert regions. Its color comes mainly from iron and it often has a purplish cast due to small amounts of manganese. It forms on exposed surfaces which are intermittently bathed with water in association with algal growth. It also forms as an alteration product of sideritic ($FeCO_3$) joint fillings when they are exposed to the atmosphere by rockfall.

DIP-The direction of inclination of a rock stratum, as given by compass bearing. For example, a stratum which dips five degrees toward the east is inclined five degrees from the horizontal plane becoming lower in elevation in an easterly direction.

DISCHARGE-The flow of a stream, measured in volume per unit time, such as cubic feet per second.

DISSECTION-Used here to mean erosional cutting by flowing water and downslope movements to form a terrain of canyons and mesas.

DISSOLUTION-The process of dissolving.

DOLOMITE-A mineral, calcium-magnesium carbonate, $CaMg(CO_3)_2$, deposited in highly saline seawater. Rock consisting of dolomite is usually called by the same name. However, it is also called dolostone.

DOME-A rock structure shaped something like a dome produced by localized uplift.

E

EFFLORESCENCE-A surface incrustation of usually soluble crystals of various kinds of salts. These form on wet surfaces in dry country as saline water evaporates.

EOCENE-The second epoch of geologic time in the Tertiary period, spanning the interval from 58 to 37 million years ago.

EROSION-The removal of weathered rock debris and of the rock itself by downslope movements, flowing water and wind.

ESCARPMENT-A steep face, like a stairstep in the terrain, such as that forming the edge of a plateau. Some escarpments may be caused by displacement of strata more or less vertically along a fault line. Others are strictly due to erosion.

EXFOLIATION-The process in which thin slabs of rock break away from steep, exposed rock surfaces.

F

FAULT-A fracture in rock along which movement has occurred so that the rock on one side of the fault has been displaced with respect to that on the other side.

FAUNA-The animal life forms of a particular place or time.

FLOODPLAIN-That part of the land beside a stream which is occasionally flooded by the stream during times of high discharge. It develops a flat aspect because mud is deposited there as floodwaters recede.

FOLD-In rocks just as in other flexible materials, a wrinkled structure.

FORMATION-A deposited layer of significant thickness and aerial extent which can be distinguished easily from underlying and overlying layers. "Formation" is a bit like the word "genus" in biology, a term of convenience in many cases, and just as hard to define.

FRONTAL-Referring to meteorological phenomena occurring at the interface between cool polar air and warm subtropical or marine air-masses.

G

GEOLOGY-The science which deals with the Earth, especially its rocks and its history of development. The term is also used to signify that which is understood concerning the Earth in a particular area, such as the geology of Zion.

GRABEN-A portion of the crust which has been downdropped by slippage on normal faults which border it on two sides. A graben need not be expressed as a valley. In fact, the Cougar Mountain graben is topographically higher than the terrain on either side because the rocks exposed in the graben are more resistant to erosion at the present time.

GRADE-The gradient at which a stream can just carry the normal load of sediment with the normal discharge. A very vague term.

GRADED BEDDING-The situation in a layer of sedimentary rock in which finer sediments overlie coarser ones, e.g. sand over gravel. Graded bedding connotes a decrease through time in the energy of the depositonal environment.

GRADIENT-The term that connotes steepness, often used for streams. A gradient of 1 percent equals a drop of 10 meters per kilometer.

GYPSUM-A hydrous calcium sulfate mineral, $CaSO_4 \cdot 2H_2O$, also known as alabaster. It is soft and easily carved. Rock strata consisting of this mineral are called by the same name. It is an alteration product of anhydrite, a mineral formed when seawater becomes increasingly saline upon extended evaporation in a closed basin.

H

HANGING CANYON-In Zion especially, a tributary canyon whose mouth lies some distance above the floor of the main canyon into which it leads. Many hanging canyons are accessible only at their upper ends. Their development has fallen behind that of the main canyons because they have disproportionately smaller watersheds. See also page 110 of the text.

HEMATITE-A soft mineral which is black when massive and "Indian" red when finely divided, composed of iron oxide, Fe_2O_3. It lends a red or pink color to the rocks. Admixed with limonite, $FeO \cdot OH \cdot nH_2O$, a yellowish hydrous iron oxide, it produces a brown coloration.

HIGH-ANGLE FAULT-A fault whose dip is greater than 45 degrees.

HOLOCENE-The most recent interval of geologic time, since the end of the last continental glaciation approximately 10,000 years ago.

HOODOO-An erosional remnant of rock in the shape of a pillar or pedestal. Hoodoos are usually capped with a rock which is more resistant to erosion than the rest of them, which causes their existence.

HORIZON-A layer of rock characterized by particular features.

I

IGNEOUS-Referring to processes involving temperatures high enough to melt rocks and to the rocks formed when the molten matter has cooled.

INFILTRATION-The soaking into the ground of rain and melting snow.

INTERFLOW CLINKER HORIZONS-Layers of volcanic cinders and clinkers, originally formed on the surface of lava flows and buried by subsequent flows.

INVERTED VALLEY-A ridge capped with volcanic flow rock. Usually the volcanic cap overlies stream gravels, indicating that the lava flowed down an ancient stream valley. Subsequent erosion has taken place on the margins of the flow (because volcanic flows are usually resistant to erosion), leaving the ancient stream bottom to stand in positive relief as the softer adjacent rocks are worn away. See also page 113 of the text.

J

JOINTS-Fractures in rock that have been formed by regional deformation; hence they run for rather long distances and tend to cut across bedding planes.

JURASSIC-The period of geologic time between the Triassic and Cretaceous periods, in the middle of the Mesozoic era. It spans the interval from 208 to 144 million years before present.

K

KARST FEATURES -Sinkholes and depressions on the land surface that are the result of the collapse of caves formed in the limestone terrain.

KULA PLATE-The oceanic crustal plate (see plate) that was located in the east Pacific Ocean and adjacent to North America in Mesozoic time.

L

LAMINA-A sedimentary layer less than 1 cm thick.

LARAMIDE OROGENY-The mountain-building episode which produced the Rocky Mountains during Tertiary and Quaternary time.

LATITE-An extrusive igneous rock which is the fine-grained equivalent of monzonite (see monzonite).

LENS-A thin-edged rock layer of limited size enclosed by strata of different material.

LEVEE-A raised embankment between a stream and the floodplain. A natural levee is formed over the centuries by the entrapment of mud in the tangle of vegetation that grows along the stream bank.

LIMESTONE-A sedimentary rock composed primarily of calcium carbonate ($CaCO_3$). It may be deposited in salt or fresh water, though the former origin is far more common, and it may consist of cemented shell fragments or lithified limy ooze.

LIMONITE-Hydrous iron oxide, $FeO \cdot OH \cdot nH_2O$, which lends a yellow or brown color to the rock when present in small quantities.

LITHIC-Pertaining to rock. Lithified means turned to stone.

LITHIFICATION-The process of being turned into stone.

M

MAGMA-Molten rock. When magma erupts from the surface, it is called lava.

MALACOLOGY-The scientific study of mollusks.

MANTLE-That portion of the interior of the Earth which lies between the crust and the core. It is about 2,900 km (1,800 miles) thick.

MARL-An unconsolidated deposit of mud or sand which consists mainly of small particles of calcium carbonate. In time crystallization converts marl into limestone.

MEANDER-A bend in a stream caused by lateral migration of the stream channel.

MEMBER-*The Dictionary of Geological Terms* (1962) has an excellent definition: "A specially developed part of a varied formation . . . [which] . . . has considerable geographic extent."

MESA-A flat-topped "mountain", smaller than a plateau and bigger than a butte.

MESOZOIC-The era of geologic time extending from 240 million to 70 million years ago.

METAMORPHIC-Pertaining to rocks that have been physically and/or chemically changed by heat and pressure. For example, when sandstone is metamorphosed it is converted into quartzite. Impure sandstone may become schist. Limestone becomes marble.

MIOCENE-The epoch of geological time spanning the interval between 24 and 5 million years before present.

MOLLUSKS-Aquatic animals of the phylum Mollusca, which includes of all things squid and octopi, but which refers here to snails and small clam-like bivalves.

MONOCLINE-A type of fold in layered rocks which has a rounded stairstep shape when viewed in cross section. Some monoclines are believed to have been formed by the "draping" of strata which overlie active normal or high-angle faults.

MONZONITE-An igneous, intrusive rock consisting of roughly equal parts of granitic and basaltic type feldspars (that is plagioclase and orthoclase) with some quarts.

MUDSTONE-A general term used to describe silty sediments which contain variable amounts of clay and sand-sized grains.

O

OLIGOCENE-The middle epoch of geologic time in the Tertiary period, spanning the interval from 37 to 24 million years ago.

OOLITE-A sedimentary rock consisting of small ovoid and spherical bodies called ooliths. Ooliths are between approximately 0.25 and 2 millimeters in diameter and thought to be formed of algal precipitates in warm, gently oscillating seawater.

OROGENY-The process of mountain building.

OROGRAPHIC-Referring to precipitation caused when moist air cools as it is forced by prevailing flow to rise over a topographic obstacle.

OUTCROP-As a noun, it means an exposure of bedrock, rock not covered by soil or other material.

OUTLIER-A separate body of a rock unit which is no longer contiguous with the rest of the unit because it has been isolated by erosion.

P

PALEOCENE-The first epoch of geologic time in the Tertiary period, spanning the interval from 66 to 58 million years ago.

PALEOSLOPE-An ancient slope, used here to mean the sloping surfaces of the land at some much earlier time.

PALEOZOIC-The era of geologic time between Precambrian and Mesozoic, spanning approximately 375 million years. The name means ancient life.

PANGAEA-Theoretical great continent (consisting of Laurasia and Gondwanaland) which began breaking apart at the end of Paleozoic time.

PECTENS-The genus of shellfish that includes the scallops.

PELECYPOD-Bivalves, that is shellfish possessing two-piece shells, like clams, oysters, scallops, mussels, etc. of the phylum Mollusca.

PERMEABLE-Having openings that permit liquids to pass through.

PERMIAN-The last period in the Paleozoic era of geologic time. It is placed between the Triassic and Pennsylvanian (Carboniferous) periods.

PETRIFICATION-The process of turning to stone, often applied to the fossilization of wood.

PIRACY-The result of headward erosion of one stream channel intercepting another stream channel. The first gains the watershed (and erosive power) of the second.

PLATE-A crustal plate is a large slab (larger than a million square kilometers) of the crust of the Earth, tens of kilometers thick, which moves as a unit in relation to adjacent parts of the crust. Elsewhere the term plate is used to mean a much smaller slab involving only part of the thickness of the crust.

PLIOCENE-The last epoch of geologic time in the Tertiary period, spanning the interval from 5 to about 2 million years ago.

POINT BAR-The portion of a stream bed located on the "inside" corner of a bend in the channel. It is the part of the bed most likely to accumulate fine sediments because of low current velocities, and a bar typically forms there.

Q

QUARTZ-The mineral silicon dioxide, SiO_2.

QUATERNARY-The most recent geological period, encompassing approximately the last 2 million years. Geologists are not in agreement on defining the point in time of the beginning of the Quaternary period.

R

RADIOCARBON-A name sometimes given to the isotope carbon-14. Carbon-14 is chemically identical to other carbon but is radioactive. All plants and animals (including you and me) contain carbon-14 unless they have been dead for tens of thousands of years. The progressive disappearance of carbon-14 from once-living matter, a result of radioactive decay, makes possible the dating of such materials, provided they are not too old.

RADIOMETRIC-Referring to the process of dating materials in the laboratory by determining how much

of certain radioactive isotopes (and sometimes byproducts) they contain.

RENIFORM-Shaped like a kidney.

REVERSE FAULT-A high-angle fault (that is, nearly vertical) caused by compression in which rock layers are thrust up and over themselves. Geologists reserve the term thrust fault for low-angle compressional faults.

RIPARIAN-The zone located along the banks of a stream.

RIPPLE MARKS-Small dune-like structures, resembling ripples, that are formed on the surface of a fine sedimentary deposit by the action of currents (wind or water) and sometimes by oscillating movement (water only).

ROCK CLEAVAGE-The property of splitting along plane surfaces that develop in some rocks as a result of internal rearrangements caused by deformational forces.

S

SAND-Loose mineral grains, usually quartz and other relatively common minerals, that are between 2 and 0.06 millimeters in diameter. Sometimes sand consists of fragments of volcanic rock (as on the beach at Waikiki) or of calcium carbonate shell fragments (on Santa Rosa Beach at Pensacola and elsewhere).

SANDSTONE-Sedimentary rock usually composed of quartz grains in the size range from 2 to 0.06 millimeters in diameter, held by an intergranular cement like calcite, quartz, or iron oxides.

SCARP-A steep slope.

SEDIMENT-The material which is deposited on the surface of the Earth, or under water, by accumulation under the influence of gravity. It would include such deposits as sand, rocksalt (an evaporation deposit) and limestone (sometimes a chemical precipitate), but not lava.

SHALE-Soft sedimentary rock consisting of clay-

size particles which splits into thin laminae.

SHEAR-To slide against each other.

SILICA-Silicon dioxide, SiO_2.

SILT-Loose mineral grains of various minerals, including quartz, that are between 0.06 and 0.004 millimeter in diameter.

SILTSTONE-Sedimentary rock composed of mineral grains in the size range from 0.06 to 0.004 millimeter in diameter, held together by intergranular cement or compacted clay.

SLICKENSIDES-The polished, grooved surface that is developed on rock surfaces in the plane of a fault by shearing motion under high confining pressure.

SLUMP-The process by which relatively large volumes of rock or unconsolidated debris move as a mass down a slope.

SPALL-To fall away, as a slab of rock separating from a vertical face and falling to the base of the cliff.

STEPPE-A vast, generally level area without forests.

STRATUM-The singular form of strata. A stratum is a layer of rock, usually a tabular volume, that is distinguished by some characteristic such as rock type, color, aspect or bedding.

STRIKE-The bearing (direction of trend) of a planar feature (rock stratum or fault zone) when projected onto a horizontal surface. Stated otherwise, the strike is 90° from the direction of dip. Beds which dip northeast strike northwest.

SUBMARINE TRENCH-Kilometers-deep, elongate troughs in the ocean floor, usually alongside continents or islands. They are zones where the oceanic crust is being thrust down underneath itself, or under continental crust, to great depths.

SYNCLINE-A fold in layered rocks which is concave upward when viewed in cross section. It is the opposite of an anticline. Synclines and anticlines are formed when the

Earth's crust is subjected to horizontal compression.

T

TALUS-The accumulation of broken rock that collects at the base of a cliff as a result of rockfall.

TEAR FAULT-A type of fault that forms in the leading edge of an overthrust plate during compression (see thrust fault). The tear faults are aligned approximately vertically and at right angles to the strike of the thrust zone.

TECTONIC-Pertaining to deformation in the crust of the Earth.

TERRACE-One type, a structural terrace, is a relatively flat terrain developed by erosion upon a relatively flat layer of rock which is resistant to erosion. Another is a relatively flat-surfaced deposit (a constructional rather than an erosional feature), usually laid down by a stream on its floodplain.

TERRAIN-Used generally to mean an area over which

the rock formations of interest are found to outcrop and produce a topographic expression.

TERTIARY-The name for the period of geologic time preceding the Quaternary period and following the Cretaceous period.

THRUST FAULT-A fault caused by horizontally directed compression in the crust in which rock strata are broken and thrust up and over themselves. The plane of a thrust fault is typically low-angle and nearly parallel to the beds that have been faulted.

TONGUE-A thin stratum of sedimentary rock lying between other strata that eventually joins a larger stratum of like rock some distance away, thickening as it does so.

TOPOGRAPHY-Pertaining to the relief of the landscape, the ups and downs.

TRIASSIC-The period of geologic time between the Jurassic and Permian periods. It is the first part of the Mesozoic era, extending from 245

million to 208 million years before present.

TRIBUTARY-A stream which flows into another stream.

TRUNCATE-Cut off.

TUFA-In this case *calcareous* tufa, a deposit of calcium carbonate at springs.

TURBID-Containing large quantities of suspended material, i.e., "muddy".

U

UNCONFORMITY-An earlier erosion surface (or surface of non-desposition) now buried by subsequent deposits. Unconformities are former surfaces of the land and often one can see ancient soils (paleosols) immediately below the unconformity.

UNIT-Used here to indicate an individual stratum of rock, anything from a lamina to a formation.

V

VARVE-A layer representing one year's accumulation of sediment.

VENT-An opening through which volcanic gases and magma break through to the surface. If a vent is active for a long enough time, a volcano or cinder cone will be formed.

ALLEN HAGOOD

Breached potholes, Clear Creek.

REFERENCES

Armstrong, R. L., and R. E. Higgins, 1973, K-Ar dating of the beginning of Tertiary volcanism in the Mohave Desert, California, Geol. Soc. of America Bull., v. 84, pp. 1095-1100.

Best, Myron G., personal communication, Brigham Young University.

Brown, Harold H., 1973, The Dakota Formation in the plateau area, southwest Utah, in *Cretaceous and Tertiary Rocks of the Southern Colorado Plateau,* Four Corners Geological Society Memoir, James E. Fassett, ed.

Cashion, W. B., 1967, Carmel Formation of the Zion Park region, southwestern Utah–a review, U. S. Geol. Survey Bull. 1244-J, Contributions to stratigraphy.

Colbert, E. H., personal communication, Museum of Northern Arizona.

Eardley, A. J., 1966, Rates of denudation in the high plateaus of southwestern Utah, Geol. Soc. of America Bull., v. 77, pp. 777-780.

Grater, R., 1945, Landslide in Zion Canyon, Zion National Park, Utah. The Journal of Geology, v. 53, no. 2 (March, 1945).

Gregory, H. H., 1950, Geology and geography of the Zion Park region, Utah and Arizona, U. S. Geol. Survey Professional Paper 220, 200p.

Hallam, A., 1975, *Jurassic Environments.* Cambridge Earth Science Series, Cambridge University Press.

Hamblin, W. K., and M. G. Best, 1975, The geologic boundary between the Colorado Plateau and the Basin and Range Province, Geol. Soc. of America Abs., v. 7, no. 7.

Hamilton, W. L., 1978, Geological Map of Zion National Park, Utah, Zion Natural History Association.

Hesse, C. J., 1935, *Semionotus cf. gigas,* from the Triassic of Zion Park, Utah, Amer. Jour. Sci., v. 29, pp. 526-531.

Hevly, R. H., 1979, Pollen studies of ancient lake sediments in Zion National Park, Utah, Proceedings of the First Conference on Scientific Research in the National Parks, v. 2, NPS-AIBS, DOI-NPS Trans. and Proc., Ser. 5, Robert M. Linn, ed.

Judson, S., and D. F. Ritter, 1964, Rates of denudation in the United States, Jour. of Geophys. Res., v. 69, no. 16, pp. 3395-3401.

Kurie, A. E., 1966, Recurrent structural disturbance of the Colorado Plateau margin near Zion National Park, Utah, Geol. Soc. of America Bull., v. 77, pp. 867-872.

Lovejoy, E. M. P., 1964, The Hurricane Fault Zone, and the Cedar Pocket Canyon-Shebit-Gunlock Fault Complex, southwestern Utah and northwestern Arizona, Ph.D. diss., University of Arizona, Tucson.

Maddox, J. Dain, April, 1977, A water resource inventory of the North Fork of the Virgin River, Zion National Park, Utah. Dept. of Forestry and Outdoor Recreation, Utah State University.

Marzolf, John E., 1970, Evidence of changing depositional environments in the Navajo Sandstone, Utah. University of California, Los Angeles.

McKee, E. D., 1952, Uppermost Paleozoic strata of northwestern Arizona and southwestern Utah, Utah Geological and Mineral Survey Guidebook, Geology of Utah, no. 7, pp. 52-55.

McKee, E. D., and S. Oriel, and others, 1967, text from Paleotectonic map of the Permian System, U. S. Geol. Survey Geological Investigations Misc. Publ. I-450, 164p.

Moir, G. J., 1964, Depositional environments and stratigraphy of the Cretaceous rocks, southwestern Utah, Ph.D. diss., University of Southern California.

Peterson, F., and G. N. Pipiringos, 1978, Stratigraphic relationships of the Navajo Sandstone to Middle Jurassic formations, southwestern Utah and northwestern Arizona, U. S. Geol. Survey Professional Paper 1045-B.

Poole, F. G., 1961, Stream directions in Triassic rocks of the Colorado Plateau, in *Short Papers in the Geologic and Hydrologic Sciences:* U. S. Geol. Survey Professional Paper 424-C, pp. C139-C141.

Rowley, P. D., J. J. Anderson, P. L. Williams, R. J. Fleck, 1978, Age of structural differentiation between the Colorado Plateau and Basin and Range Province in southwestern Utah: Reply, Geology, v. 6, pp. 572-575.

Stewart, J. H., F. G. Poole, and R. F. Wilson, 1972, Stratigraphy and origin of the Chinle Formation and related Upper Triassic strata in the Colorado Plateau region, U. S. Geol. Survey Professional Paper 690, 336p.

Winnett, T., 1978, K-Ar dating of Quaternary basalts, Zion National Park, Utah, senior thesis, The Ohio State University.

INDEX

ABOUT THE AUTHOR

❖ Wayne L. Hamilton has a long association with National Parks and Southwestern Utah. Born in Kanab, Utah, in 1936, he was raised in a National Park Service family and lived in Grand Canyon, Saratoga National Historical Park, the Natchez Trace Parkway, and Yellowstone as a child.

❖ He studied geology at Dartmouth College and worked seasonally in Yellowstone during college years. After serving with the Army Corps of Engineers in Greenland and northern Alaska, he became involved in research on such topics as the growth of sea ice and development of a method for dating cores from polar ice.

❖ He received his Ph.D. in 1969 at Ohio State University, where he taught, conducted research on problems such as the transport and fate of pollutants in urban ecosystems, and explored relationships between Earth tides and volcanic activity. In 1972, he joined the faculty of the Geology Department at Cleveland State University and became involved in full-time teaching.

❖ In response to his long-standing love affair with National Parks and the National Park Idea, he resigned his teaching position and in 1974 rejoined the National Park Service in Zion National Park. He subsequently worked at the N.P.S. Denver Service Center as a geologist and as coordinator for physical science research in Yellowstone National Park.

❖ Since 1983 he has been engaged full-time in a variety of research programs, including geothermal investigations and assessment of unrest of the Yellowstone Caldera—a potentially explosive volcanic system.

Photograph by Gilbert Dewart.